P9-DNW-997

Praise for *When Faith is Forbidden*

During my two years imprisoned in Turkey, one of the things that strengthened me was looking to the example of others who persevered faithfully through persecution. There is a long line of people who have suffered for Jesus Christ. Some struggle more than others—I certainly did—but in the end what matters is to stand. Stories like the ones Todd has collected in this book are of great value as we prepare ourselves in case we are called on to stand in that long line—and I believe it is a matter of great urgency that we indeed prepare.

PASTOR ANDREW BRUNSON | Former prisoner for Christ in Turkey

It was with a great deal of anticipation that I read *When Faith Is Forbidden*. It did not disappoint. His book removes the reader from that of an observer who stands comfortably outside of the lives of persecuted believers. This book moves us from a place of pity for those who suffer for expressing their faith in the marketplace to an active stance of true partnership. Todd invites the reader inside the narrative by shining a light on believers for whom persecution is normal. His written prayers, wedded to these very personal accounts, offer opportunities for personal reflection and growth. Significantly, the reader is encouraged to capture and record their own thoughts as persecuted believers lead us into a life of faith where witness and persecution are twins. I pray that readers will use this book to enhance their service for Jesus. *When Faith Is Forbidden* is a God-sent gift for families who are looking for a devotional aide that will enrich times of family worship.

NIK RIPKEN | Mission veteran of 35 years; author of *The Insanity of God*

When believers in the West sing "I have decided to follow Jesus," we rarely consider what the cost of that commitment might be. But for many Christ-followers around the globe, that decision could cost them their lives. It's imperative we hear the stories of the persecuted church. It provides us with the precious privilege of praying for our brothers and sisters and it sweeps away the cobwebs of complacency in the Western church. Get your passport, fasten your seatbelts, and travel with Todd to get a global perspective of what it means to follow Jesus. Your faith will never be the same again.

JANET PARSHALL | Author and nationally syndicated talk show host

As a leader in the Middle East I have firsthand experience of seeing Todd taking a story about persecution and being able to conceptualize it for broad audiences to understand and engage. I have personally known him for over a decade and he has been recording our stories for years and even used a few in this beautiful book. Every time I read Todd's stories I am inspired and lit on fire once again to suffer well in the persecuted world. I am thankful for how he has given his life to documenting stories like these because they will not only touch you, but they will allow the Holy Spirit to start a beautiful work in your life. How can you light your faith on fire in the slumber of North America? How can you overcome the spirit of apathy? I believe his book will give you hope and fire to fulfill the call in your life.

ANONYMOUS CHURCH LEADER IN THE MIDDLE EAST

Todd's latest book *When Faith Is Forbidden* is truly inspiring and transformative. In nearly two decades of field ministry among the persecuted part of the body of Christ, Todd has lived among and sometimes through them. It's also transformative because these stories are not just testimonies, but more importantly they show that God gives life, smiles, and joy, even when His persecuted faithful are suffering because they do not conform to the world. Every Christian who desires to live a godly life in Jesus should read this book.

BOB FU | Founder and President, China Aid Association and former prisoner for Christ in China

I have known Todd Nettleton for many years—and he can tell a story! What better stories for us to hear than those of triumphant saints during our lifetime. Thanks to Todd, these "victory stories" are no longer unknown. They are brilliant, and they have moved me to PRAY!

GRACIA BURNHAM | Ethnos360 missionary, author of *In the Presence of My Enemies*

While reading *When Faith Is Forbidden*, I felt like I was walking on holy ground. The stories in this riveting book take you deep into the heart of some of the most dangerous countries in the world for Christians to live in. But the overcomers that Todd Nettleton writes about don't merely survive in persecution, they thrive in it. Christ has been so formed in them they have become an unstoppable force for the kingdom of God. Thank you, Todd, for taking us on this thrilling forty-day journey! I love this book and highly recommend it. How inspired I was to meet these brothers and sisters who are more than willing to suffer and give their very lives for Jesus. Our Savior is amazing and so are these saints who follow Him no matter the cost!

TOM DOYLE | Uncharted Ministries CEO and coauthor with JoAnn Doyle of *Women Who Risk: Secret Agents for Jesus in the Muslim World*

I believe that the Lord has uniquely positioned and commissioned Todd to write this book. The Bible tells us that the persecution will increase as we approach the end times—yes, even in Western countries such as the USA. As a matter of fact, it has already started. So for us living in the West, the story-based devotionals in this book not only strengthen our faith to walk more closely with the Lord, but they also prepare us to respond properly to the persecution some of us are facing today (2 Tim. 3:12), and all of us will face tomorrow (Matt. 24:9).

HORMOZ SHARIAT | IranAlive.org

Connecting the dots between current events, people who are nameless and faceless, and your heart can be difficult. Even hearing stories of the persecuted church, while sympathetic, our hearts are not pierced. We often sing "break my heart for what breaks Yours" in worship, but do we understand what that means? Reading through *When Faith Is Forbidden* will take you through a journey that might do that. The stories remind us of who God is and what He is doing through the chaos around the world; they will remind us of our state of Body, all the while revealing God's fingerprints in our own lives. If nothing else, be encouraged by what's happening worldwide because these stories reveal the wind is blowing change to all corners. You'll be challenged to pray, not only by these stories but also by Todd Nettleton's reflections, as well as your own. This project could be "The Faith Challenge." I don't think you'll come out of it the same person you were when you went in if you wholeheartedly participate over the next forty days in prayer.

RUTH KRAMER | Executive Producer and anchor of Mission Network News

For Jesus, for the apostles, for the church triumphant and at rest, for the church militant and missionary, and for our brothers and sisters around the world . . . suffering always precedes glory. The cross-less, pain-less, suffering-less Christianity the West has (off and on) experienced for the last three hundred years is an extended aberration that is soon coming to an end. *When Faith Is Forbidden* reminds us both of what is normal Christianity and what is our common future in these last days before our Lord Jesus returns.

DICK BROGDEN | Cofounder of the Live Dead Movement, Jeddah, Saudi Arabia

As a family, we remember the persecuted in prayer as often as possible, understanding the biblical truth that when one part of the body suffers, we are called to suffer with them. Now, in the pages of this book, we have the unique opportunity to meet them! Travel with Todd to China, the Middle East, Africa, and other places, and sit down with Christians who joyfully sacrifice *everything* to follow Christ. The stories of their faith will challenge your faith. Take this 40-day journey to meet and be inspired by other members of our spiritual family.

BENJAMIN WATSON | Author, activist, former NFL tight end

WHEN FAITH IS FORBIDDEN

40 DAYS
ON THE FRONTLINES WITH PERSECUTED CHRISTIANS

TODD NETTLETON
with
 The **Voice** of the **Martyrs**

MOODY PUBLISHERS
CHICAGO

Some content in this book has been adapted from the author's work published originally by The Voice of the Martyrs in VOM's print magazine and online.

Unless otherwise indicated, all Scripture quotations are from the ESV® Bible (The Holy Bible, English Standard Version®), copyright © 2001 by Crossway, a publishing ministry of Good News Publishers. Used by permission. All rights reserved.

Scripture quotations marked NKJV are taken from the New King James Version. Copyright © 1982 by Thomas Nelson. Used by permission. All rights reserved.

Scripture quotations marked NASB are taken from the (NASB®) New American Standard Bible®, Copyright © 1960, 1971, 1977, 1995, 2020 by The Lockman Foundation. Used by permission. All rights reserved. www.lockman.org

While all the events in this account are factual, some names and identifying details have been changed for security purposes.

Edited by Kevin P. Emmert
Interior Design: Puckett Smartt
Cover Design: Erik M. Peterson
Cover photo of caseside graphic copyright © 2011 by FreeTransform / iStock (115905400).
Cover photo of journal with paper copyright © 2016 by gurkoao / iStock (504182338).
Cover illustration of passport stamps copyright © 2019 by Fourleaflover / iStock (1165723077).
Cover illustration of Middle East stamps copyright © 2019 by LifeofRileyDesign / iStock (1185821355).
Cover illustration of stack of photos copyright © 2012 by crossbrain66 / iStock (171580669).
Cover illustration of world map copyright © 2016 by lukbar / iStock (599273638).
All rights reserved for the photos/illustrations above.
Author photo by Corey Lack

All websites and phone numbers listed herein are accurate at the time of publication but may change in the future or cease to exist. The listing of website references and resources does not imply publisher endorsement of the site's entire contents. Groups and organizations are listed for informational purposes, and listing does not imply publisher endorsement of their activities.

Library of Congress Cataloging-in-Publication Data

Names: Voice of the Martyrs (Organization) | Nettleton, Todd, author.
Title: When faith is forbidden : 40 days on the frontlines with persecuted
   Christians / The Voice of the Martyrs and Todd Nettleton.
Description: Chicago : Moody Publishers, 2021. | Includes bibliographical
   references. | Summary: "Spend forty days getting to know your persecuted
   brothers and sisters. With When Faith is Forbidden, you'll journey with
   the Christians who risk their lives to follow Jesus. Each daily
   devotional includes inspiration and encouragement through the story of a
   persecuted believer"-- Provided by publisher.
Identifiers: LCCN 2020035796 (print) | LCCN 2020035797 (ebook) | ISBN
   9780802423061 (hardcover) | ISBN 9780802499462 (ebook)
Subjects: LCSH: Persecution--Biography. | Spiritual journals--Authorship.
Classification: LCC BR1608.5 .W44 2021 (print) | LCC BR1608.5 (ebook) |
   DDC 272.092/2--dc23
LC record available at https://lccn.loc.gov/2020035796
LC ebook record available at https://lccn.loc.gov/2020035797

Originally delivered by fleets of horse-drawn wagons, the affordable paperbacks from D. L. Moody's publishing house resourced the church and served everyday people. Now, after more than 125 years of publishing and ministry, Moody Publishers' mission remains the same—even if our delivery systems have changed a bit. For more information on other books (and resources) created from a biblical perspective, go to www.moodypublishers.com or write to:

Moody Publishers
820 N. LaSalle Boulevard
Chicago, IL 60610

3 5 7 9 10 8 6 4 2

Printed in Korea

For Charlotte:
Every story told in these pages, every trip to Bangalore, Beijing,
or Baku, meant days you were a single parent and nights you slept
alone. Yet you continually sent me out, entrusting me to God's
care, commissioning me for His work, and praying for me as I
went. I've seen your sacrifice. Our Father has seen it, too.
These stories are the fruit of *our* ministry—for you are and have
been a full partner every step of the way.

For those willing to live for Christ, no matter the cost:
I hope, dear reader, you desire inclusion on that list. He is worthy!

CONTENTS

DEPARTURE DAY:

PREFLIGHT CHECKLIST

These all died in faith, not having received the things promised, but having seen them and greeted them from afar, and having acknowledged that they were strangers and exiles on the earth. For people who speak thus make it clear that they are seeking a homeland. If they had been thinking of that land from which they had gone out, they would have had opportunity to return. But as it is, they desire a better country, that is, a heavenly one. Therefore God is not ashamed to be called their God, for he has prepared for them a city.

HEBREWS 11:13–16

....

We're leaving for the airport in twenty-five minutes. I hope you're ready.

I'm rushing around my house, trying to figure out how to get my suitcase closed and which things in it I won't actually need on the trip. I check my phone again to see what the weather is predicted to be: the warm jacket takes up a lot of suitcase space. Will I need it? Will I need a nicer pair of shoes for church? Is anyone going to expect me to be wearing a tie?

Every extra item prompts a tiny cost-benefit analysis. *Yes*, it would be nice to have my running shoes in case the hotel has a fitness center. But they take up precious space. Yes, I'd love to have my personal Bible, but my traveling New Testament is *much* smaller and lighter—and I have the whole Bible on my phone if I need it. And I always hope to have a little bit of *extra* space when I leave, because invariably I come home with a small souvenir for my wife or a gift for my sons (when they were young, their favorites were swords, knives, or any sort of weapon!) and daughters-in-law.

As the son of missionaries, I grew up in a traveling family. The packing rules were simple: if you can't carry it yourself, you can't bring it. This was sometimes tested, such as when we carried silverware for twelve to Papua New Guinea—in our carry-on bags! I still try to follow that rule: one medium-sized checked bag and one carry-on, which has my camera, headphones, and eBook reader, as well as various and sundry power-adapter cords and hopefully a snack and a spare shirt, because there's never a guarantee your suitcase will arrive the same time you do.

Our ride should be here in ten minutes. Can you push down right here while I zip my suitcase closed?

Early on in my time at The Voice of the Martyrs, I had a very different idea about visiting persecuted Christians. I remember on my first VOM trip to China, our team was going to meet a pastor who'd been arrested multiple times in the previous three months. He led a large unregistered church that met on Tuesdays, and police and Religious Affairs authorities had taken to arresting him each Tuesday morning so he couldn't lead the services. They'd hold him all day, or even overnight, then let him go, just so he couldn't lead his growing flock.

So as we went to visit, I had a picture in my mind of this poor, abused pastor. I thought how much of a blessing it would be to him for foreigners to come and cheer him up, because he'd no doubt be feeling deeply discouraged. My ideas couldn't have been much further from reality!

When we arrived at his apartment, he was smiling and joyful. He was thrilled that people in his area were meeting Jesus Christ, thrilled his flock was growing. If the price of effective ministry was a few measly arrests or a few nights in jail, then so what? It was worth it to see lives changed and Christ's kingdom grow.

I remember clearly how he showed us the bag he took with him to church: it had a blanket and a change of clothes. It was his jail bag, and he was packed and ready to go.

I turned to his wife, sitting to the side as we sipped cups of tea. "Don't you worry about him?" I asked, pointing to the pastor.

"Why should I be worried?" she answered through the translator. "God will take care of him."

God will take care of him. And God will take care of us.

Since that trip, I have different ideas about my travels. While persecuted Christians greatly enjoy fellowship with other believers, they don't *need* me to cheer them up. In fact, often in their presence, I wish for much more of the joy that shows on their faces and in their lives. I go to hear their stories. I go as a learner, wanting to know more about their faith and their walk on their journey toward home—"a better country, that is, a heavenly one." And when I get back to my earthly home, I want to tell the story of their amazing faith.

Will you peek out the window to see if our ride is here?

As you begin reading this book, we're going on a journey together. We're going to spend forty days experiencing what it's like to travel into restricted nations and visit people like that brave Chinese pastor and his wife. I'm glad you're coming along with me to hear the stories of some of those I've met over the past twenty-three years.

But if you're a follower of Christ, you were on a journey before you opened this book. In several places, like the passage we started with today, the Bible talks about Christ's followers as visitors, foreigners, exiles and even "aliens" here on earth. We're not home here, because we're not of this world. We're only traveling, heading toward our real home: heaven.

So as we take this journey together to meet persecuted Christians, I hope we learn some truths for our other, more important, journey: the one that will take us to heaven.

As we're leaving for the airport, here's the first lesson: pack lightly.

Many Christians are journeying through life carrying more baggage than they should be. Instead of one checked bag and one carry-on, they're trying to take six checked bags and three huge carry-ons. They load up a cart to push through the airport, but then they can't even see where they are going to push the cart! They're thinking more about where they are now than about their final destination, and they're carrying way too much. And, just as the airlines charge a passenger for "overweight bags," these believers are paying a price for carrying too much weight.

Maybe your extra bag is un-forgiveness; you're carrying a grudge that's making your bag too heavy. Maybe it's unconfessed sin. Perhaps you're carrying too many material possessions that keep you from thinking enough about our real home. Maybe it's busyness; your schedule is so packed you can't even take time to enjoy the places you're visiting.

There's our ride, pulling into the driveway.

As we head to the airport, and as we depart for this journey together, will you prayerfully ask God to show you if you're carrying too much through your life's journey? I hope the testimonies of our persecuted family members will bless and challenge you. And I hope they'll make you think more about our true home, and about the path you're on to get there.

Passport? Check.

Itinerary printout? Yes.

Money? Check.

OK, we're ready.

Pat the dog, kiss your spouse and kids.

Let's go.

FOR REFLECTION

How often do you remember that you are a "stranger and exile" on this earth and that your ultimate destination is "a better country"? How does that knowledge affect the way you will live this day? Are you packing lightly for the journey through this life on your way home? Are you carrying anything you don't need, that serves only to take up space and make your bags too heavy?

As you consider these questions, write answers for your journal (below). What needs to happen for you to lay those things down and leave them behind?

PREFLIGHT PRAYER

Lord God, please go with us on this journey. Please soften my heart for the people we'll meet along the way and use them to show me more of Your truth. Remind me often of the "better country," my real home, and escort me safely throughout this trip until You bring me there. Please show me if there are things I'm carrying that I shouldn't be, and help me to lay them down.

For Your Journal

_____

_____

_____

_____

_____

_____

_____

From My Journal

October 19, 1998 (right before leaving on my first trip
for VOM, to Sudan).

One week from tomorrow, I will be leaving my nice,
safe, comfortable life in Bartlesville to spend ten days
distributing food and Bibles in Sudan . . . about ten
thousand miles outside my comfort zone.

It has been interesting, the ways I have thought about
this trip and what might happen. First, I had to think
about the possibility that I won't come back. Sudan is
a dangerous place, and quite honestly the government
soldiers there wouldn't hesitate to put a bullet in my
pale, American body.

Knowing I might not come back has given special
urgency to my days here. I want to spend every moment
with Char and the boys, being an exemplary husband
and father. I want to be caring and compassionate. I
want to turn off the TV and spend more time talking and
listening. I want to hug a lot, and tell them each I love

them about twenty-five times a day.

But then I felt guilty. Why don't I live like that all the time? Why does a trip to Sudan scare me into being the man I should be 365 days a year? Do I feel vulnerable in war-torn Africa but think I'm indestructible in America? Do I not know that a drunk driver or drive-by shooter or random act of violence or car wreck could end my life tomorrow, right here in America? Why don't I always live ready to die instead of only when I'm getting ready for an international trip?

Perhaps that is the lesson of this trip for me. Not to take tomorrow for granted, but to live each day ready to step off planet earth and into eternity.

DAY 1

BEYOND OUR CONTROL

The heart of man plans his way, but the LORD establishes his steps.

PROVERBS 16:9

....

Yei, Sudan, 1998

It's not unusual, your first day overseas, to be wide awake at 2:30 or 3:00 in the morning. I've heard lots of theories about how jetlag can be beaten, but so far I don't find any that actually work. Jetlag just keeps beating me. During the day, get as much sunlight as you can. Other than that, you just have to fight through it.

Our team wasn't supposed to go to Yei first during our time in Sudan. But the first lesson of travel is that, sometimes, things don't go according to plan. Our goal was to go to Turalei.

It was in Ayien, a village near Turalei, that Pastor Abraham Yac Deng had led a church of four hundred Sudanese Christians—with his small red pocket Bible, the only copy of the Scriptures in the entire congregation. Abraham had been thrilled when a previous VOM team brought boxes and boxes of Bibles to Turalei. The thought that every family in his church could have their own copy of the Bible was almost too amazing to consider.

A member of the VOM team asked Abraham what his favorite verse was, and he quoted Romans 6:23: "For the wages of sin is death, but the free gift of God is eternal life in Christ Jesus our Lord."

Four days after that conversation with Abraham and those Bibles being delivered, radical Islamic *mujahidin* attacked Ayien. The just-delivered Bibles were burned, over twenty people were kidnapped from the village, and Pastor Abraham was shot in the head.

The team I was part of, months after that brutal attack, planned to replace the destroyed Bibles. But heavy rains in Turalei have flooded the airstrip at both ends, and the pilots aren't sure the dry part in the middle is long enough to land—and then take off again—with the twin-engine Russian Antanovs we've chartered for aid delivery.

So our team leader decided to switch the order of our trip. We'd come to Yei first. Hopefully we could get to Turalei in a few days. Except now we're in Yei and we can't find a ride. We have Bibles to take to the SPLA (Sudan Peoples' Liberation Army) troops closer to the battle lines, but the truck we thought we'd rent isn't available. There's another vehicle available, but they're waiting on a delivery of fuel. We're staying with very kind missionaries who are taking wonderful care of us, but we are most definitely *not* accomplishing what we set out to.

Finally, we found other mission workers heading our way and joined them. But, two hours into our trip, the bridge over an unmapped river was out. Our lead vehicle plunged in, attempting to ford the river. They made it halfway across before the rain-swollen rush of water began to slide the four-wheel-drive truck downstream. Our teammates climbed out the window onto the roof of the vehicle, and we were able to throw them a rope and stop the truck from sliding any farther, as well as give them a (wet) way back to shore.

So instead of handing Bibles to soldiers near the front lines, we're stuck here waiting for the river to go back down so we can retrieve the other truck.

What are you doing, Lord? We're on Your side! We want to replace Bibles the enemy destroyed. Couldn't You at least stop the rain long enough for the airstrip to be dry? Couldn't You at least arrange so we could get a truck when we needed one? Couldn't You keep the river levels low enough that we could cross?

Of course, God can do anything He wants to do. He can stop rain or make it rain. He can dry up rivers or make them overflow. But on my trip to Sudan, nothing seemed to happen according to our carefully laid plans. Why?

I wish I could tell you. I wish I could point to some significant milestone result from our trip and say, "See, *that's* why God let the rains come." I wish I could point to some soldier we handed a Bible to—in a place we didn't plan to be—who went on to become Sudan's Billy Graham. We did deliver Bibles, even though some of them had to be laid out in the sun to dry before being read. We did deliver food, in one case taking high-protein mix to a "hospital" (you and I would probably call it a clinic) caring for dozens of malnourished kids. We fellowshipped with the missionaries who hosted us, and I hope we blessed and encouraged them.

But, due to circumstances beyond our control, we didn't accomplish the goals we set out to achieve.

Beyond our control. Those aren't words I like. I want to be in control. I want to make decisions. I want to make a plan and then work with others to see it come to fruition. I want to know the outcome. I want control!

But, once we choose between cornflakes or toast for breakfast, isn't most of the rest of the day beyond our control? Isn't the whole point of the Christian life to *give up* control to a loving, holy Father who will organize our journey through life for our greater good? As Solomon tells us, we plan our ways, but it is the Lord who establishes our steps (Prov. 16:9). Do you believe that? Do I?

It's easy to get frustrated at all the things beyond our control. A flooded airstrip. A plane that doesn't show up on time. A whole town that doesn't have any gas for sale.

Or, closer to home, a job situation that doesn't go according to plan. A doctor telling you it's going to require more tests to be sure. A child consistently choosing an ungodly path.

Life is beyond our control. Death is beyond our control. So, we have to adjust. We have to be ready to cheerfully change course. We must allow His timing to trump our plans. And we won't always know why. *Why* is for Him to figure out. It's beyond our control.

FOR REFLECTION

Are there areas in your life where you're trying to exercise control, but you need to acknowledge are beyond your control? What are those areas? What would it require for you to surrender the need to be in control?

For your journal, write about one of those areas, and what it will look like as you surrender control of that part of your life this week to your loving Father and allow Him to establish your steps.

PRAYER

Father, I admit I want to be in control. I want to make my plans and have You bless what I want to do. Help me trust You to see what I cannot see. Help me surrender my need for control and allow You ultimate control, to trust Your plans are for my greater good. Help me each day to seek Your face and Your will, and allow You to work in and through me to accomplish Your purposes for me and those around me.

For Your Journal

From My Journal

October 31, 1998, Yei, Sudan (addressed to my wife, Char)

. . . I am praying for you, though. I have asked God to send angels to surround our home and protect [it] from the attacks of the enemy or anything else that would cause grief.

The rest of the story: one of the nights I was in Sudan, my wife—who was sick while I was gone—woke up in the middle of the night. Looking up from the bed, she saw clearly the outline of men's shadows on the mini-blinds covering the two windows of our bedroom. She got up and looked out each window, but couldn't see anyone outside. Yet instead of fear, she felt a sense of complete peace, and immediately got back into bed and fell back into a deep, restful sleep.

She and I both believe in angels.

DAY 2

"I USED TO BEAT HIM"

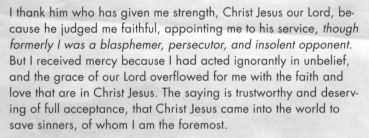

I thank him who has given me strength, Christ Jesus our Lord, because he judged me faithful, appointing me to his service, *though formerly I was a blasphemer, persecutor, and insolent opponent.* But I received mercy because I had acted ignorantly in unbelief, and the grace of our Lord overflowed for me with the faith and love that are in Christ Jesus. The saying is trustworthy and deserving of full acceptance, that Christ Jesus came into the world to save sinners, of whom I am the foremost.

1 TIMOTHY 1:12–15

....

Near Allawa, Ethiopia, October 2005

The nickname "Haji" is a term of respect in the Muslim world, bestowed on those who have completed their *hajj* pilgrimage to Mecca, one of Islam's five pillars. It's not commonly combined with the title pastor!

We met "Pastor Haji" at his grass-roofed house in the southern part of Ethiopia, an area where a rising tide of radical Islam was threatening the church and Christian believers. Outside the house, there was a burn mark on the wall. One week prior, radical Muslims tried to set fire to Haji's house. Thankfully, he put out the fire.

As we sit, drinking orange sodas Haji graciously offered us, we can look up to see sunlight streaming through holes in the tightly packed grass roof. The holes are the result of neighborhood Muslims throwing stones onto the house, trying to pressure Haji and his family to leave the area or return to Islam. Thankfully, none of his family was injured by falling stones.

Haji understands the hatred of radical Muslims. He used to be one of them! He was so devout, he was sent to Saudi Arabia for special training.

As we stood outside the hut, Haji had his arm around the evangelist that brought us to meet him. Nodding his head toward the evangelist, he said five words I will never forget.

"I used to beat him."

What?

"I used to beat him." Haji went on to tell us that he was the leader of a radical Islamic group of young men, and part of their holy duty to their Prophet was attacking and harassing Christians. One of those they attacked was this very evangelist, the man now smiling with Haji's arm draped loosely across his shoulders.

In spite of beatings, the evangelist refused hatred for his attackers. Instead, he showed them love and offered them blessings and good news. Haji had no explanation for such a response. How could a man you were beating show love to you? How could he not grow angry and fight back?

Eventually, Haji's heart was won by the gospel message and the love of the Christian man he was attacking. He left the vitriol and violence of Islam for peace beyond his understanding.

Islamic friends were not happy with his decision. Haji would spend a year in jail. He would face some of the same tactics he'd used against Christians. Now he was facing rocks through his roof and attempts to burn down his house. But he would not give up his faith in Jesus.

Once again, I'm struck by the *joy* the men and women of our persecuted Christian family possess. Haji is a happy man. His smile is huge. His laugh comes easily and often. This is not a man who lives in constant fear, though the threats against him are real and constant. This is a man having fun, living an adventure, and serving a great King.

Haji is having kingdom impact. Who better to talk to Muslims about Jesus than a former Muslim, one who completed the *hajj*, one so devout he was sent to Saudi Arabia for special training? Who better to spell out the differences between a god who will weigh out your good deeds and bad deeds to see whether you've earned the right to enter paradise, and a God who knows our good deeds can never outweigh our sinfulness, and so sent His own Son to pay the price for our bad deeds and purchase our entrance to heaven with His own blood?

Haji's story is not unique. One of the church's first great missionaries was a man so zealous for his religion he asked for the assignment of hunting down men and women who didn't follow their teachings. Then that man ran into the very One he was persecuting, and was forever changed.

One of our VOM contacts in Colombia has a saying: "A racehorse can run just as fast in either direction." One who is zealous for sin will often become zealous for Christ. One who beat Christians might eventually accept beatings with joy in service to his King.

It's easy for us to look at someone with holier-than-thou religious eyes and write them off spiritually. He is so hard-hearted nothing could reach him. She is so trapped in sin she can never get out. But the testimony of Pastor Haji—and the apostle Paul—is that *none of us* is beyond the reach of God's grace and mercy. And those saved from much are often the racehorses that run fastest for Christ and furthest to reach others for Him.

"I used to beat him," said the pastor. Said the persecuted Christian. Said the kingdom worker. With a smile.

FOR REFLECTION

Are there people you've written off spiritually, people you've decided God should give up on reaching? Who, in your circle, is "a blasphemer, persecutor, and insolent opponent" of Jesus and His good news? Perhaps that's the very person God is calling you to love and reach. Perhaps God has plans for them to be a Paul—or Haji—who will do great work for His kingdom. How can you respond to them in such a way that Christ's love will shine through you?

Write down that person's name and steps you'll take *this week* to begin establishing a bridge by which to deliver the gospel.

PRAYER

Father, in my own strength I cannot love this person. Sometimes I can't even stand to be in the same room with them! Please give me Your love for them. Help me see them how You see them, and send the Holy Spirit to soften the soil of their heart.

For Your Journal

_____

_____

_____

_____

_____

_____

_____

_____

From My Journal

We also met twelve MBB [Muslim Background Believers], young people who've been kicked out of their homes by their parents. They are now living with Christian families who have taken them in, and trying to go on with their education. It costs only $4 to $5 per month for their housing and food!

Can you imagine your own parents kicking you out of the house? One girl today had that happen at age thirteen—literally kicked out on the streets!

We also met a couple of guys whose wives left or kicked them out when they became believers.

PRAYING FOR PERSECUTED CHRISTIANS

One of the most important conversations new believers in Christ from a Muslim background (like our new Ethiopian friend, Haji) ever have is the first time they tell someone close to them they are no longer a Muslim, but now a follower of *Isa al Masih*—Jesus the Messiah.

That conversation can lead to our new brother's or sister's murder.

It can also open a doorway to share the gospel.

PRAY TODAY for new believers all over the Islamic world deciding when and with whom to have that vital conversation.

DAY 3

"WE HAVE EVERYTHING WE NEED"

Not that I am speaking of being in need, for I have learned in whatever situation I am to be content. I know how to be brought low, and I know how to abound. In any and every circumstance, I have learned the secret of facing plenty and hunger, abundance and need. I can do all things through him who strengthens me. . . . And my God will supply every need of yours according to his riches in glory in Christ Jesus.

PHILIPPIANS 4:11–13, 19

....

Outside Irbil, Northern Iraq, January, 2016

We're sitting in a tent in a displaced-persons camp in Northern Iraq. ("Displaced persons" are people who had to flee their homes, but have not crossed a national border. "Refugees" are people who fled their homes and are now outside their home country.)

As ISIS washed over the Nineveh plains, tens of thousands of people—Christians, Yazidis, Shia Muslims and even ISIS's fellow Sunnis—fled in front of them. As of our visit to northern Iraq, most were living in tents in camps. The camps are segregated: Sunnis here, Shias there, Christians in that section over there. The tent we are sitting in is in the middle of the Sunni section—one thousand-plus Sunni families all around.

Our host in the tent is a man named Mohammed. I love Christians named Mohammed! It's January, and it's cold outside. It snowed a couple of days previously; now the dirt tracks in the camp are shoe-sucking mud. And the wind, which seems to come from every direction, is piercingly frigid. A little kerosene stove knocks a bit of the chill off inside the tent, but I never took my coat off the whole time we were there.

Mohammed and his wife are from Mosul, the largest city in Northern Iraq and at that time the largest city ISIS had conquered. He was a Sunni Muslim when, about ten years before our meeting, he had a dream in which Jesus Christ came and spoke personally to him. When Mohammed woke up, he made the decision to follow Christ—the One who would come and speak personally to him.

At first, Mohammed's wife was very upset that her devout Sunni husband would become an apostate, an infidel. How could he turn his back on the true faith? But, about three months later, she had the *very same dream* Mohammed had described to her. Jesus came and spoke to her, personally. When she woke up, she made the same decision her husband had: she, too, would follow Jesus.

After hearing Mohammed's testimony, I asked his wife if she saw changes in her husband after he had that dream. "Well," she said, through our translator, "he stopped beating me." *Certainly*, I thought, *a good first step in a man's walk of faith!*

Having been saved by Christ, Mohammed began to tell others in their neighborhood in Mosul. Now he wasn't just an apostate himself; he was actively encouraging other Muslims to also become apostates. Their house was burned down. Police promised an "investigation," but, unsurprisingly, no suspects were ever found. Mohammed and his family moved to a new house, and began to talk about Jesus to the neighbors there.

In 2014, with ISIS about to take the city, Mohammed knew he must get his family out. ISIS wouldn't just burn their house down. They would give Mohammed one chance to return to Islam, then execute him when he didn't. The family fled Mosul, eventually coming to this camp near Irbil. Because Mohammed's ID card still said "Sunni Muslim," he and his family were sent to this tent in the Sunni camp.

But the camp wasn't 100 percent Sunni anymore. Since their arrival, Mohammed and his family had led people from two other families to Christ. Even in the camp, they were witnesses. Given two UN-issued tents on their little concrete slab, Mohammed and his family (they had five children) decided to live in one tent and reserve the other for prayer and Bible study meetings. They were already having an impact, but that impact wasn't unnoticed. Mohammed told us that either he or his wife stay with the tents at all times; they fear Sunnis angry about their faith might destroy the tents if they leave.

As foreigners, our presence draws attention; we can't stay long. After hearing Mohammed's testimony, I asked him, "What are you praying for? What are you asking God for?"

He spoke, then the translator said, "We don't have to ask God for anything. We have everything we need. We are happy!"

My first thought was to argue with Mohammed.

Come on, now, Mohammed. You live with five kids in a tent! Some of your neighbors would like to kill you! How can you possibly think you have everything you need?!

In that moment, I think the Holy Spirit said something like,

Listen more. Talk less.

There is great truth in what Mohammed said. *We have everything we need.* We have a roof over our heads. We have food for today. And we have a mission field in every direction, right outside our door. What more could we ask for?

Mohammed and his family live in *daily* reliance on God. "Give us this day our daily bread." They live that prayer every day! They are living what the apostle Paul wrote, that he'd "learned in whatever situation I am to be content."

I find this—living in daily reliance on God—a personal challenge. I think many Americans find this challenging as well. We are, after all, the help-yourself country. Pull yourself up by your bootstraps! If you work hard, you can do anything. And I love that can-do attitude that's part of the American ideal.

But what about living in daily reliance on God? What about, instead of "I can do all things through my will and effort," we learn to be content—we live "I can do all things through Christ, who strengthens me"?

FOR REFLECTION

What is it that you live in daily reliance on? Is it your paycheck, your job, your smarts, your family? Or is it God? Do you count on Him for *all* your needs, from a roof over your head to the right words to say in every conversation?

Write down the person or thing you are relying on most in your life, then write what it would look like for you to live in daily, moment-by-moment reliance on God.

PRAYER

Lord Jesus, I recognize that I often rely on _____
more than I rely on You. Forgive me! Help me put my faith in
You, not only in a lifelong and eternal way, but also in a daily,
moment-by-moment reliance on Your plan and Your provision
for me and my family. Help me see the steps You have ordered
before me today, and thank You that, in You, I have everything
I need.

For Your Journal

_____

_____

_____

_____

_____

_____

_____

From My Facebook Post That Day

When I asked Mohammed, "What are you praying for? What
are you asking God for?" he said: "We don't need to ask for anything. We have everything we need! We are happy."

Sometimes I wonder if I even have ANY quality at all that could
be called faith.

If you ever wonder why I do this work and fly halfway around
the world . . . it is for opportunities to sit in tents with Jesus-followers
like this man and his family. I can't wait to come home and share
that story!

DAY 4

"I ALMOST DROWN TAKING A SHOWER"

But when he saw the wind, he was afraid, and beginning to sink he cried out, "Lord, save me." Jesus immediately reached out his hand and took hold of him, saying to him, "O you of little faith, why did you doubt?"

MATTHEW 14:30–31

....

Hussein, Part 1: Undisclosed Country, 2009

Hussein is not his real name. He lives in Iran, but we met in another country willing to grant visas to both Iranians and Americans.

Hussein grew up in a strict Islamic home. His mother was a devout Muslim, reading the Quran and praying five times each day in the prescribed fashion. His father was not as devout, but if anyone suggested he wasn't a very good Muslim, he would become angry, even violent. He beat Hussein's mother. Their marriage teetered on the brink of divorce.

After completing mandatory military service, Hussein returned home. Jobs were hard to come by; instead of finding one, he joined an old friend in a counterfeiting operation, a crime punishable by death under Iran's strict penal system. But he and his friend didn't get caught, and Hussein's income went up and up and up. His was a life of debauchery: women, drugs, parties. Such activities might numb his pain for a moment, but none filled the emptiness he sensed inside himself.

He and his friend had a disagreement, and Hussein found himself out of the counterfeiting business. Suddenly, his income was zero. But his drug addiction didn't end when his income did.

Hussein was miserable. He began to make plans to kill himself. "I wanted to die," he told me, "but I didn't want it to hurt." He decided to get high on ecstasy, then jump off the roof of a tall building. He found an appropriate building, and even a way to sneak up to the building's roof. Now all he needed was the drugs.

While he was looking for this final score, an old army buddy called Hussein. He would be visiting Hussein's town and hoped to meet up. Over coffee, Hussein's buddy said he had found *something new*.

Hussein's ears perked up. What he thought he heard was that his friend had discovered some new drug, and Hussein was certainly looking for drugs. Instead, his friend told him he had found Christ.

That friend sent Hussein a New Testament, and he read the book of Matthew. But that first reading didn't make much sense to him. When his friend came back to town, he brought other Christians to meet Hussein. They met in a local park on a beautiful, sunny day. One of them, a woman named Padina, had also struggled with drugs and depression and had also made a plan to kill herself. The Christians really listened to Hussein and sympathized with the pain in his life.

Looking him right in the eye, Padina asked if Hussein would like to give his pain to Jesus.

Hussein didn't feel like he had anything to lose; if Jesus didn't work out, he reasoned, he could still decide to kill himself. Why not pray with them? What could it hurt? But when he prayed to Jesus and asked Him to take control of his life and to take all his pain, something amazing happened. Instantly, he felt lighter. Hussein told me that he felt "unexplainable happiness" after praying to receive Christ.

Hussein's life began to change. He quit drugs, drinking, and cigarettes. Seeing the dramatic change in his life, both his brother and sister accepted Christ. Church leaders noticed Hussein's witness and identified him as a potential leader in the church.

Hussein sensed God's call to further ministry. He fought against it, though, trying hard to tune it out. With God's help he'd beaten addiction and rebuilt his life. He had a good, legal job. He had a car and a house. He was willing to serve the Lord—partly. Couldn't he serve the Lord *and* keep his comfort and steady income? The church group could even meet at his house!

Eighteen months later, Hussein was part of a group of Christians that went on a retreat to the sea.

The sea wasn't really Hussein's favorite spot. He told me sarcastically just how good a swimmer he is: "I almost drown just taking a shower!"

But as he stood on the beautiful beach, the water seemed calm and shallow, and he stepped in. And then he stepped out a little farther, and a little farther still. The tide dragged him out, and Hussein found himself underwater, clawing for the surface, terrified. In his panic, he silently cried out to God, admitting that he didn't want to die because he had never answered that call to work *wholly* for Him. The man who once planned to jump off a tall building now didn't want to die without answering God's call!

God answered his prayer. Hussein described it like feeling hands lift him to the surface and hold his head out of the water.

Seeing his panic, three lifeguards went in and pulled him out, saving his life. Afterward, as he shivered in a blanket on the beach, they told him, "We could see that you had your head up out of the water, so we knew you were a strong swimmer. If you hadn't been such a strong swimmer, we never would have gone after you because you would have dragged us down."

Hussein just looked at them. He was thankful for their help, but he knew what had *really* happened: God had saved him from certain death.

Hussein answered God's call to full-time ministry. When he first told the church leaders, they told him he was emotional from his near-death experience; they advised he wait and pray about it for a few weeks before making a final decision. Hussein insisted that he was ready to give up *everything* to serve the Lord. He quit his job, even after his boss offered him a promotion. He sold his car and paid his debts and prepared for a new life. The leaders saw his resolve and began his training. For thirty days, he went out with a church leader and his wife, simply watching what they did.

Immediately, God began to confirm Hussein's call. As they walked into one house where they were ministering, the daughter in the family began to cry. When she calmed down, she told them that the night before, she saw Christ in her dream, and He led her to a table where she sat down with three people. And now those *same three people* had come into her home! For her, it was confirmation of the truth of the gospel; for Hussein it was a confirmation that God had called him and would bless his ministry.

FOR REFLECTION

Have you ever argued with God? Perhaps you sensed His call to do something more or deeper than what you were doing, but worried that answering His call would mess up the life you were comfortable with. Perhaps you're wrestling with Him *even at this moment.*

Write down what's holding you back, that attitude or possession or lifestyle you don't want to surrender. Don't wait until the waves are over your head or the opportunity has passed; God's plan is for your *best.* Say yes—right now!—to the next thing He's asking you to do.

PRAYER

Lord Jesus, forgive me for the times I choose my comfort over Your calling. Help me to say yes the first time You ask, to put Your kingdom ahead of my comfort. Help me say yes to You and Your plans for me.

For Your Journal

_____

_____

_____

_____

_____

_____

_____

_____

_____

From My Journal

Padina and her husband are here. Padina is a woman that I interviewed in [withheld for security] in 2004, and wrote about in *Iran: Desperate for God.* Her mother was

SO THRILLED to meet me and thanked me so much for writing Padina's story.

She also said what I'd written was just "Chapter One," that there's a lot more of her story to write now.

DAY 5

"WHICH ONE OF THOSE IS BAD?"

For I know that through your prayers and the help of the Spirit of Jesus Christ this will turn out for my deliverance, as it is my eager expectation and hope that I will not be at all ashamed, but that with full courage now as always Christ will be honored in my body, whether by life or by death. For to me to live is Christ, and to die is gain.

PHILIPPIANS 1:19–21

....

Hussein, Part 2: Undisclosed Country, 2009

Ministry in Iran comes with a cost, and it wasn't many months into his full-time ministry life that Hussein was holding a Bible study in an apartment when police raided. Hussein and the believers had just received a shipment of five hundred Bibles stacked in three large boxes in one of the rooms. The police searched the entire apartment and threw everything into the middle of the living room floor. Even pictures were pulled off the wall and thrown into a pile. Hussein said one policeman even picked up a needle lodged between two floorboards. Yet, miraculously, they *did not notice* three large boxes of Bibles sitting in the middle of the bedroom!

Police still arrested Hussein and his two female coworkers. They drove him to a large prison, then blindfolded him, put him in another car, and drove him somewhere else. Hussein was wondering what to say, and questioning a bit why he'd given up his good job and comfortable life.

The guards led him to a solitary confinement cell, which measured ten feet by six feet. A huge floodlight lit the room twenty-four hours a day. When Hussein asked to turn it off, a guard said, "What do you think this is, a hotel?"

Hussein's mind was a raging storm of questions. What had his female coworkers admitted? What should he tell police? How long would he be held? And what would his parents think when they learned their son was in prison?

Sitting on the hard floor in that solitary cell, Hussein encountered Jesus Christ. Hussein told me he heard God speak the same way you or I hear water running when we turn on a faucet. He said, "I felt like Jesus put everything aside, the whole world aside, to come to me and whisper in my ear." Hussein began to pray. All his desperate questions faded away. God's peace filled him completely, filled up the entire cell.

He sensed Christ asking him, "Why are you worrying about what you're going to say? There is no need for *you* to decide what to say because I'm going to tell you what to say."

Hussein's fear was gone.

Interrogations began. Hussein had prayed he wouldn't have to lie, and God arranged so he could answer every question truthfully. He was interrogated every day, but none of the policemen ever asked if he was a Christian, if he'd actually left Islam to follow Christ. When they asked about "the Bibles," Hussein assumed they'd found the five hundred Bibles he knew were in the bedroom at the apartment. But he was careful how he answered their questions, trying to say as little as possible. Later he learned the interrogators were talking only about the *two* Bibles in his backpack.

After a few days, he was taken to court. He stood before the judge and, like the interrogators, the judge never asked if he was a Christian. Hussein was returned to solitary confinement, where he would spend a total of ten days. There was no bed, and at night, guards would throw water into the cell to make the floor wet, so Hussein couldn't lay down and sleep.

After another week they transferred Hussein to a regular prison and sent him to Level 11. He learned that Level 11 was for death row prisoners. When he got there, the guard said, "Don't bring him here, the other prisoners will kill him!" But the paperwork said Level 11. The guard opened the gate, Hussein went in, then the guard closed it. Hussein was behind the gate, amidst 250 death row inmates; the guard was on the other side of the gate. Behind that gate, Hussein learned, prisoners run everything—the entire death row area is controlled by a gang.

Hussein prayed and wondered what to do. That night, leaders of the gang ordered him to come with them. He was frightened, imagining terrible things they were about to do to him. But God was working. Somehow, the gang leaders had heard that Hussein had contacts in America. They wanted him to tell the outside world how terrible the conditions were in the prison. By the end of the meeting, Hussein had been accepted into the leadership of the gang—one of the top eight leaders out of the 250 death row inmates! He slept on a top bunk his very first night on death row, when people who had been there five years were still sleeping on the floor! He had a private shower. He had fresh fruit and vegetables every day. He was in charge of distributing water, so all of the prisoners were nice to him because they wanted to be sure to get their allotment of water! God not only protected Hussein, He put him into a position of authority!

(Perhaps you want to pause here and read, or re-read, the story of Joseph in Genesis.)

Hussein said death row was like a hotel to him. Two days after he arrived, the guard offered him a transfer to a "safer" part of the prison. Hussein turned it down, saying he'd rather stay on death row!

He spent ten days there, then was released on bond. He still had to come back to that city for his court hearing, but when he did, he found God working there too. When Hussein entered the courtroom, the judge, wearing the long beard of a devout Muslim cleric, looked furious. But when Hussein's case came up, the judge's countenance changed. Hussein showed him the appeal document, and the judge said, "No, this is wrong. Let me change it." He literally filled out Hussein's appeal document! The judge told Hussein the procedure to file the appeal, where to go to file the documents, and where to deliver them. And he said if Hussein had any trouble, to just give him a call, and he'd help move things along.

Later, the judge told Hussein he didn't even have to show up for the court hearings—the judge would take care of it.

Miracle, miracle, miracle, miracle. It seemed that at every step of Hussein's spiritual journey, God had a miracle waiting.

I asked Hussein if, in light of all of these miracles, he was ever afraid. "No," he said. "I've seen God work so many times already. What do I have to fear?"

Hussein is continuing in ministry in Iran. He knows there will be other encounters with police. I asked if he was worried.

"I think one of two things will happen," Hussein told me. "They will either kill me, or there will be another miraculous event like these."

Then he smiled and asked, "Which one of those is bad?"

FOR REFLECTION

Hussein saw his life as two choices: continue to live on earth and see God work miraculously on his behalf or go immediately to heaven. "Which one of those is bad?"

Sometimes, we need to refocus on the "better country" that awaits us. Paul instructed the Colossian church to "Set your minds on things that are above, not on things that are on earth" (Col. 3:2). How will you focus today on heaven, eternity in Christ's presence, and the glory we will experience after we are done being "strangers and exiles" on earth? It's easy to have our eyes locked on today, this week, this year. But eternity is what matters! Walking in fellowship with Jesus here on earth is wonderful, but it is *nothing* compared to eternity in the home He's prepared for us.

Write down ways your view of *now* could be blocking your view of eternity with Christ. How can you refocus your eyes and your mind on the "things that are above"?

PRAYER

Jesus, help me hold loosely my life here on earth and understand more deeply the glory I will experience when I enter Your presence, so I can say, with Hussein and the apostle Paul, that "for to me to live is Christ, and to die is gain" (Phil. 1:21).

For Your Journal

_____

_____

_____

_____

From My Journal

After that I met with "Hussein" again to finish his testimony. His story is amazing! Seriously! Like Joseph-in-Egypt amazing! He was in jail—and they put him on death row—where the serious, hard-core criminals were. The guard said, "This is a mistake. They're going to kill him!"

By the next morning, he was accepted by the gang that ran things, and put in charge of delivering water to all the prisoners. He had a private shower, fresh fruit—like a hotel!

He said it was like God said, "I TOLD YOU I could take care of you!"

Hussein said that his Bible hero is Samuel—because he heard God's voice so clearly.

QUOTES TO CONSIDER

Read your New Testament again and you will agree that mediocrity in the Christian life is not the highest that Jesus offers. Certainly God is not honored by our arrested spiritual development—our permanent halfway spiritual condition.

We all know that the Bible tells us that we honor God by going on to full maturity in Christ!

Why, then, do we settle for those little pleasures that tickle the saintlets and charm the fancy of the carnal?

It is because we once heard a call to take up the cross and, instead of following toward the heights, we bargained with the Lord like a street huckster! We felt an urge to be spent for Christ, but instead of going on, we started asking questions. We began to bicker and bargain with God about His standards for spiritual attainment.

This is plain truth—not about unbelieving "liberals"— but about those who have been born again and who dare to ask, "Lord, what will it cost me?"

—A. W. Tozer[1]

Beloved, do not be surprised at the fiery trial when it comes upon you to test you, as though something strange were happening to you. But rejoice insofar as you share Christ's sufferings, that you may also rejoice and be glad when his glory is revealed. If you are insulted for the name of Christ, you are blessed, because the Spirit of glory and of God rests upon you. But let none of you suffer as a murderer or a thief or an evildoer or as a meddler. Yet if anyone suffers as a Christian, let him not be ashamed, but let him glorify God in that name.

1 Peter 4:12–16

DAY 6

"THAT HOPE KEPT ME STRONG"

Cast your burden on the LORD, and he will sustain you; he will never permit the righteous to be moved.

PSALM 55:22

....

Nepal, 2012

It was a long, hot drive to the tin-roofed house in southern Nepal where our VOM team met Danmaya. The air conditioner in our taxi couldn't quite keep up with the heat, and we alternated between running it full blast to try to stave off the swelter and rolling down the windows to let the hot, steamy air blow across our sweating faces. When we arrived at our destination and ducked into the brick house where Danmaya lives, it was even hotter than our taxi, like one of those brick pizza ovens only with plastic chairs inside.

It's not Danmaya's house; she just lives there. The house actually belongs to her pastor. He and his family live there, too.

The house has only one room.

The pastor welcomed us and pointed me to a plastic chair. He sat on the one bed in the room. His wife sat on the floor. He shared some of his testimony, then talked about Danmaya.

When a Christian friend shared the gospel with Danmaya six years before we met her, it was impossible for her to know how much it would cost to follow Jesus. Danmaya willingly received the gospel, the good news, and committed her life to following Christ. She was weary of trying to please the millions of Hindu gods, and she felt in her heart the truth of God's love demonstrated through Jesus Christ.

When she told her husband, he didn't think her faith would last. He told her to keep it to herself so she wouldn't bring shame on their high-caste Hindu family. But Danmaya's faith didn't stay the same. It grew, and soon it was too large to keep to herself. Eventually, it could not be contained in their simple home. About a year after she first accepted the gospel message, Danmaya asked to be baptized. Now her husband knew this wasn't a fad or phase his wife was going through. She wasn't going to hide or keep quiet that she was no longer a Hindu; she was a Christian, and soon everyone would know.

"This is not our custom," he told her. "Give up your faith. Otherwise I will leave you. I don't want you being with me since you are a Christian and I am a Brahman (high-caste Hindu)." Eventually, he threw Danmaya's possessions outside. She was no longer welcome in her own home. Later, he took a new wife.

In Nepali culture, it's customary for an abandoned wife to return home to her parents, or to the home of an older brother, where she will be provided for. But Danmaya's own parents would not take her back unless she renounced her faith. Where would she go?

Jesus warned His followers that "a person's enemies will be those of his own household" (Matt. 10:36). Danmaya experienced the truth of His promise. She wouldn't deny Christ, though her unwavering commitment to Him cost every family relationship she had in the world. But through these losses and the fear for her future—

Where would she go? Who would provide for her?—God granted Danmaya a sense of peace and His presence.

When her earthly family kicked her out, her spiritual family opened their doors and took her in to the small brick house we sat and sweated in.

Hearing Danmaya's story, I suspect it's easy to picture a down-trodden, angry woman left in homeless desperation by her husband. But when I met this childless, deserted woman, she glowed with the joy of the Lord. She doesn't consider being crammed into this stifling brick house a consolation prize. She considers it pure joy (James 1:2).

How has she stayed strong in her faith through such trials?

"Whatever persecution comes—even if I die—I will be *alive* with Christ in heaven," she told our team. "That hope kept me strong."

Forgiving her husband was a process for Danmaya, and not an easy one. "In the beginning, I had a kind of bitterness in my heart [toward him]," she said. "But later, I came to know that unless I forgive him, I cannot go the right way to God. So I have forgiven."

Today, she prays for her former husband, and even for the woman he's now married to, asking God to draw both to Himself.

We asked Danmaya if there was a particular Scripture that gives her strength. She turned to Psalm 55:22: "Cast your burden on the Lord, and he will sustain you; he will never permit the righteous to be moved."

FOR REFLECTION

I am often floored by the high price our brothers and sisters in hostile and restricted nations are asked to pay for following Christ, when I and so many Christians in the US are asked to pay so little. I'm even more amazed when they pay that price not grudgingly, or with frustration or disappointment, but with a pure, unfiltered *joy*.

Perhaps these brothers and sisters have grasped a truth that we need to be reminded of. The privilege of walking with Christ, forgiveness of sin, the promise of heaven—that privilege is worth *everything*. Think of the parable of the treasure in the field: the man who found the treasure sold *all he had* to own it. But he didn't do so hesitantly; he sold it all "in his joy" (Matt. 13:44).

Does your life and walk of faith exhibit that same joy? Are there cares and burdens weighing on you? What are they? Are you willing to "cast" those burdens onto the Lord?

PRAYER

Lord, thank You for giving me salvation, for allowing me to be a part of Your kingdom! Remind me that this inestimable gift is worth more than everything I possess on earth—even my family. Help me serve You with the same joy with which Danmaya serves, in spite of challenges or hardship that may come along the way.

For Your Journal

_____

_____

_____

_____

_____

_____

_____

_____

_____

_____

From My Journal

She [Danmaya] has given up everything—yet she had a wonderful, joyful smile on her face and just radiated the peace and joy of the Lord.

The flight here was amazing! Mount Everest was behind us, so I don't think we saw it. But we did see some <u>HUGE</u>, <u>HIGH</u> mountains of the Himalayas. So high that we looked <u>UP</u> at them out of the airplane window!

DAY 7

DRIVEN TO BE THE BEST—PART 1

Therefore, if anyone is in Christ, he is a new creation. The old has passed away; behold, the new has come.

2 CORINTHIANS 5:17

....

Turkey, 2010

Some people have a competitive fire that burns so brightly its heat drives everything they do. My new Iranian friend, Iman, is one of those people. But before he would tell me his story, he paused to pray.

He said he didn't want to even *think about* the things he did before he met Christ; he didn't want to give Satan even a crack in the door to influence his life. So he prayed that God would bring back only the things He wanted Iman to share and that He would protect him from the memories and influence of the ways Satan had controlled him before he met Jesus.

Iman started his story by talking about the competitive fire that drove him his whole life. When he was a soldier fighting in the Iran-Iraq war, he told his commander to send him to the place where the fighting was the fiercest, the place where he could be a martyr for his country within twenty-four hours.

And when he was a thief, he was driven to be the *best* thief, stealing things other thieves had tried and failed to snatch.

And when he was a drug addict, he wanted to be the *best* drug addict. He wanted to use every drug available, and he wanted to use more of each drug than anyone else was using.

Whatever he was doing, he was driven to be the very *best* at it.

As a young man, Iman was involved in a terrible car accident. The car was totaled, yet he walked away without even a scratch. People who saw the accident told him how amazing it was that he'd been able to steer the car around the obstacle, to maintain control of the vehicle. But Iman knew that wasn't him; he hadn't been steering. He credited the spirit of his martyred brother, who had died in the war. Or maybe it was his mother's prayers to Allah on his behalf. Only years later would he find out Who rescued him that day.

Once drug addiction sank its ugly, poisonous teeth into Iman's flesh, he didn't much care about anything. Not his family. Not eating. Nothing except the burning, all-consuming question of where his next fix would come from. He was on his way to being a statistic; one more in a long line of Iranians who'd lost hope and turned to the needle for comfort.

One night, high on drugs and flipping through channels, Iman came across a Christian satellite TV channel. He was on the station only a few seconds, but the words he heard somehow stuck in his mind: "When I gave my heart to Jesus . . ."

Wow, he thought. *Christians are very strange people to actually give their hearts to somebody. These days, people won't give away even a pen* [my translator explains that the Farsi words for *heart* and *pen* sound similar], *and Christians are giving their hearts! That's crazy!*

Ten days later, he was drunk and again flipping channels. Once again, he flipped across the same Christian TV channel. It was on the screen only a few seconds, and the only words he heard was a lady saying, "When I gave my heart to Jesus . . ." He changed the channel, again thinking how crazy Christians must be to give away their hearts.

His family was planning a fun trip out of town, but Iman's addiction was so strong, and he looked so terrible, they invited him *not* to make the trip with them. He was devastated; even his own family didn't want to be seen with him.

That night, he was up on the roof of his house, smoking crack. The drugs were almost gone, and Iman was feeling the weight of the misery of his life. He realized he was powerless against the pull of drugs. "I couldn't even imagine that I could live without drugs for even one day. Because I had tried before to be free from drugs and had failed."

In desperation, Iman looked up at the sky and said, "God, save me. Save me from my addiction."

In that moment, he was brought back in his mind to the car accident fifteen years earlier. Suddenly he knew Who it was that had steered the car and brought him through that experience: it was God.

Iman fell to his knees and lifted his hands in prayer, thanking God for saving him all those years earlier, repenting of not giving God credit for His miracle then, and begging to be saved from his addiction.

"I expected to hear a voice, or that I might see a light. I didn't see that, and I was really disappointed. I went back to sleep in my bed, but before I went to sleep I said, 'God, it doesn't match Your character to let me go empty-handed. Either You are not real or I am too sinful for You to do anything for me.'"

He got in bed, but turned on the TV, again flipping through channels. This time when he came across the Christian channel, he paused a little longer.

It was the same sentence again, "When I gave my heart to Jesus . . ." But this time, Iman stayed on the channel to hear the rest of the sentence: ". . . He saved me."

Two hours before, Iman had prayed on the roof for God to save him. Now he heard the way God would do that: when he gave his heart to Jesus.

Iman was suddenly glued to the TV. The person sharing his testimony on the screen had also been a drug addict, had also been hopeless. But, looking at his face, Iman could see no sign of drugs. The man looked completely clean. And he looked joyful! Then the pastor came on the screen and said to everyone watching: you can have this same joy, this same healing, this same victory.

Iman prayed again, repenting completely of every sin in his past, giving his whole heart to Jesus.

"When I closed my eyes to pray I felt the presence of Jesus beside me, 100 percent. I felt if I had opened my eyes at that point I would have seen Him. I was too ashamed of myself and my sins to open my eyes. As a sinner I don't deserve to see Him, but my feeling was telling me, 'God is here!'"

When he opened his eyes, Iman sensed a Power inside him saying, "It is finished. Your old life is finished." Iman was a new creation.

Iman had wanted to be the best soldier he could be, even to die as a martyr for his country. And then he'd wanted to be the best thief, and then the best drug addict. Now he'd found Christ, and that competitive fire was turned in a new direction. He wanted to be the best! The best witness for Christ, the most loving disciple, the most joyful!

If he was going to follow Jesus, he was going to be the *best*.

FOR REFLECTION

You may not have been a drug addict or a thief before you met Jesus, but it is still a miracle that He saved you. Sometimes I believe it is good to remember what we were—and where we were destined to end up—before Jesus saved us. Not in a way that gives Satan a foothold, but in a way that reminds us of the joy and thankfulness we felt when that old life was put away and we became a new creation. Write down your "new creation" story, and ask God to give you an opportunity this week to share it with someone.

PRAYER

Jesus, thank You for saving me! I didn't deserve it; I never could have earned it, and yet You rescued me from sin and hell. Thank you! Help me serve You joyfully out of love for You and thankfulness for all that You've done for me.

For Your Journal

_____

_____

_____

_____

_____

_____

_____

From My Journal

It is very cool to be around people who are really sold out for the Lord and giving their lives for His work.

DAY 8

DRIVEN TO BE THE BEST—PART 2
"THE SWEETEST TIME OF MY LIFE"

> And Jesus went throughout all the cities and villages, teaching in their synagogues and proclaiming the gospel of the kingdom and healing every disease and every affliction. When he saw the crowds, he had compassion for them, because they were harassed and helpless, like sheep without a shepherd.
>
> **MATTHEW 9:35–36**

....

Turkey, 2010

From the night Iman committed his life to following Jesus, he's been an evangelist. Not only on Sundays or in front of crowds of people; he sees *every single person* he comes into contact with as a person God has brought into his path to hear about Jesus. Just as Iman wanted to be the best thief and the best drug addict, now he wants to be the best evangelist.

"I don't evaluate the value of people according to earthly values; every person for me is valuable because of Jesus. In every situation, I ask the Holy Spirit, 'What do You want me to do?' So I am available to share the gospel."

That availability produced amazing results. The first time I met Iman, he had been a follower of Jesus for four years. And in that four years he had knelt and prayed with more than 1,000 people as they renounced their life of sin and committed their hearts and lives to following Christ. More than a thousand people!

He became part of a network of Christian leaders in Iran, receiving training and accountability from those in leadership of the network. Like others in the network, every month he sends a report of his work that month, including how many people he spoke to about salvation in Christ and how many people chose to follow Jesus and prayed with him.

Of course, Iman lives in a restricted nation—the *Islamic Republic* of Iran. So this daily ministry talking to people about Jesus is going to draw attention. It's going to end up getting him arrested, interrogated, and maybe even sent to prison. But Iman's attitude is, *If I'm in prison, it must be because someone here needs to hear about Jesus.*

"When they arrested me for no reason, I just knew God was sending me to a place to witness. So, I didn't fight so they would take me to jail. They took me to the jail, and I saw two people who were bound because their crimes were very serious. When I came to those people, I told them, 'God has sent me to save you.'

"So by faith, I believe that those who are around me, God has sent for me to share the gospel. So I shared the gospel very briefly, just about in 15 minutes, and they knelt and prayed to repent and receive Christ.

"I only had those 15 minutes to share the gospel because after I shared the gospel, immediately after, the police came and said, 'You have been very good, and you shouldn't be here. You are very kind to us and we want to release you.' They opened the door and said I could go.

"When they opened the door to release me, I hugged those two criminals and they were crying and hugging me really hard. So the warden of the police was like, 'You have only known these people for 15 minutes, and they act like you are family!'"

Iman's passion to reach sinners with the message of salvation through Jesus rubbed off on many of those whom he witnessed to and prayed with. One man Iman led to Christ began by talking to his father, who was a member of the security police. His father feigned great interest, saying, "That's very interesting. I would love to meet with your friend who shared this message with you."

So the son invited Iman to come back to his city, and to meet his father. However, when Iman arrived at the meeting, the police were waiting. He was arrested, blindfolded, and put into a car. At the police station, he was interrogated for more than ten hours, then taken before a judge.

Standing before the judge, Iman shared his testimony of coming from addiction to freedom in Christ. He told the judge that from that day forward, every time he saw a drug addict, he wanted to talk with the person to let them know there was hope and freedom available to them. He wasn't trying to build a political movement or even plant a church; he was simply acting out of his thankfulness that God had saved him from drugs, and he wanted others also to be rescued from addiction.

At the end of the hearing, the judge sent him back for further interrogation. The first night Iman felt great fear. He was sure the guards were planning to sexually assault him. He cried out to God.

"I learned to focus on the presence of Jesus. I said, 'Whatever happens, it is worth it for what You did for me.' I learned what it means to wrestle with God because at that point I told God, 'Even if they rape me I will not renounce You.'"

At first, when Iman began to pray in the cell, the guards told him to stop. "I've been with you all day," he responded. "I've answered every question you asked. But you can't take prayer from me."

"Those prayers," he told me later, "in the cell were so sweet. Whenever I prayed, I would just cry. The sweetness was that I knew I wasn't there because of things I had done wrong. That made my prayers very sweet, because I knew I was there because of God."

Iman would pray for the guards who brought his meager food. He would pray God's blessings on their lives and marriages and families. Soon, guards were sneaking extra food to him.

For twenty-one days, Iman was in solitary confinement. Then guards moved him to a larger jail, among four hundred other prisoners. Iman was sent to one of the worst cells, a room full of murderers, addicts, and mentally ill prisoners. Through a friend with influence at the prison, he was offered to change rooms. He declined. "If God is sending me to that room, I don't want to be anywhere else," Iman said.

In his cell there were sixty-five people, but only forty-five beds—fifteen triple-decker bunk beds in a twenty-by-twenty foot cell.

A fellow prisoner asked if Iman had just arrived at the jail. "No, I was in solitary confinement for twenty-one days!"

"How did you survive being all alone? I was in solitary for six days, and I almost went crazy!"

"Oh, I wasn't alone," Iman told him. "I was with God."

"I want to talk to you," the other prisoner said. And so launched Iman's prison ministry. That same day, he laid hands on a drug addict going through withdrawals, praying for him in Jesus' name, and the man's symptoms were healed.

There were three cameras monitoring the room, so Iman's ministry had to be stealthy. He would go under beds to talk to other prisoners out of sight of the cameras.

"It was the sweetest time of my life," Iman told me. He was in the cell for eight days. He saw twenty-four fellow prisoners come to faith in Christ. Two were convicted murderers awaiting execution. On the fifth day, Iman was told he could put up bail money and be released; he delayed making the bail payment for three days to continue his ministry in prison—until the guards grew suspicious about why he wasn't leaving.

"I believe that when God sends us to some place, He prepares and equips us for that place," Iman told me. "I knew I had a mission in that prison."

After he was released and back home with his family, Iman filed his normal monthly ministry report to his leaders. He didn't mention arrest, twenty-one days in solitary confinement, or time in prison— just ministry work: "In the past month, I was able to share the gospel with one hundred people. Of those, twenty-four prayed for the forgiveness of sins and committed their lives to following Jesus Christ."

It was only several weeks later that his leaders realized Iman's ministry that month had happened *inside a prison.*

"The day I was out of jail, I continued my ministry," Iman told me. "Until my last breath, I owe Jesus. Whatever I have done, it was the Holy Spirit in me. I know who I was. I was so weak before, so all the glory goes to Jesus. I am nothing; Jesus is everything. Without Jesus, I am the same [sinful, addicted] person that I was before."

FOR REFLECTION

What place of ministry has God prepared and equipped you for today? Where is He sending you? Who is it that He's placing in your path? Do you see *every* conversation and *every* person you meet as someone God sent to you to hear about His love and His grace? If you see people, as Jesus did, through eyes of compassion, how will it change the way you interact with those around you?

PRAYER

Lord, allow me to see those around me through Your eyes of compassion, and not through my own human eyes. Allow me, this very day, to speak of Your love to someone You place in my path. I am ready to be Your minister, Your ambassador. Guide me to that person who, right now, needs to hear from You.

For Your Journal

_____

_____

_____

_____

_____

_____

_____

_____

From My Journal

Had a really good interview with an evangelist who . . . spent about a month in prison, including 21 days in solitary confinement. But in his month in prison he led 24 people to Christ! And even after his bail was arranged he stayed three extra days to disciple and keep witnessing—until the guards started to wonder why he wasn't leaving yet!

He made an interesting comment: "If you're a Christian and you haven't been persecuted, you're really missing out on a blessing!"

PRAYING FOR PERSECUTED CHRISTIANS

I'll never forget a conversation with Bob Fu, a former prisoner for Christ. I asked Bob how he prayed for imprisoned Christians before he himself was put in prison for his ministry activities in Communist China. He said that, before prison, he prayed imprisoned Christians would be released and allowed to return to their families.

I asked him if, after he spent time in prison himself, he prayed *differently*.

Yes, he said. Now he prays imprisoned Christians will have opportunities to witness for Christ, and that God will sustain them as long as it is His will for them to be in prison.

PRAY TODAY for imprisoned Christians. Pray for their protection and health. But also be sure to pray for opportunities—this day—for them to witness to someone about Jesus' love. Perhaps it will be a fellow prisoner, or a prison guard, or even a judge. But pray God will give them opportunity, and then courage and grace to take advantage when that opportunity to witness comes.

DAY 9

PERSECUTION IS THE EXPECTATION, NOT AN ACCIDENT

"If the world hates you, know that it has hated me before it hated you. If you were of the world, the world would love you as its own; but because you are not of the world, but I chose you out of the world, therefore the world hates you. Remember the word that I said to you: 'A servant is not greater than his master.' If they persecuted me, they will also persecute you. If they kept my word, they will also keep yours. But all these things they will do to you on account of my name, because they do not know him who sent me."

JOHN 15:18–21

. . . .

India, 2010

Bangalore is sometimes called "the IT capital of India," a tech hub where most of the world's well-known technology companies have a presence. It was there, in India, I heard one of the "freshest" stories of persecution I've ever heard, interviewing a persecuted pastor just twelve hours after he was released from prison.

Peter Paul bears the names of two apostles, and just as Peter and Paul preached about the risen Jesus, Peter Paul also preaches that gospel message, wherever he is.

Peter Paul supplemented his tiny pastoral paycheck working as a teacher. While India is a predominantly Hindu country, the slum area where Peter Paul lived and worked was predominantly Muslim, and most of his students came from Muslim families.

Peter Paul founded an after-school tutoring program to help children academically, but also as a point of contact for outreach to introduce them to Jesus. He handed out copies of the *JESUS* film to many of his students, and they happily took the discs home and shared the film with their families.

That act of evangelism somehow flew under the radar, but his next step did not: Peter Paul gave New Testaments to about twenty of his young students.

The students didn't have shelves full of books at home, and they were very proud of the brand new books they'd been given. But when they took the New Testaments with them to the madrassa where they received Islamic instruction, its leaders were incensed. Why were Muslim children being given Christian books? They demanded to know who'd given the children the books.

Leaders of the madrassa gathered a mob of about 150, recruiting angry Muslims from three local mosques. They all went to Peter Paul's house, arriving just as Peter Paul was finishing his morning prayer time.

Dragging him outside, members of the mob slapped and kicked Peter Paul, chanting repeatedly that they wanted to kill the infidel.

Peter Paul's wife, Nirmala (alas, not Mary), tried to negotiate with the mob. She promised her family would leave the area if only they would release her husband. Peter Paul told his wife not to worry.

"I said to my wife, 'Whatever is the Lord's will will happen in my life,'" he told us. "I did not feel afraid. I knew God could redeem me from them."

Members of the mob ransacked the family's house, destroying everything inside. Then they dragged Peter Paul to the school where he taught, calling local police and the media to the scene of his "crime"—telling people about Jesus.

When police came, they didn't arrest members of the mob who had just beaten a man and destroyed all his possessions. Instead, they arrested Peter Paul, citing him for "disturbing communal harmony" by giving Christian books to Muslim kids. He was taken to jail.

Pastor Peter Paul told me that while he was in jail he thought about the Bible stories of God's children being locked in jail. He thought about Paul and Silas, singing in stocks in the jail in Philippi. He thought of the story of Peter, bound between two Roman soldiers when the angel arrived and led him out of the prison.

He began to pray. But his wasn't a prayer for rescue or release.

"Whatever is Your will," he told the Lord, "do it in my life."

Peter Paul asked the prison leader if he could speak to the other prisoners, and when permission was granted he stood up and shared his testimony of God's work in his life. He preached about giving glory to God in every circumstance.

"Wherever we are," he told his fellow inmates, "we should give glory to God. When we are in the trials and temptations. When we are having all the good things, also. All the time we should give glory to God." After his message, several inmates sought him out and asked to pray with him.

VOM coworkers were able to hire a lawyer to represent Peter Paul, and provided funds to bail him out of jail. So it was that after almost a week in jail, he was released on a Saturday night. We sat down with him and Nirmala over steaming cups of tea on Sunday morning. Their two beautiful children were still sleepy-eyed and not quite awake.

They had no place to go. During the week Peter Paul was in jail, their landlord decided his family was too much trouble and that, as long as they lived in his house, it was possible the mob would come back and ransack it again, or even burn it down. He didn't want to risk his property, so he evicted Nirmala and the children even as Peter Paul was in jail.

Peter Paul was out on bail, but the charges against him were still pending. There was a significant chance he would go back to jail. As he and Nirmala sat with us and sipped tea, the clothes they wore were the sum total of everything they owned in the world. The family's earthly possessions had been destroyed. They had no home to go back to. They weren't sure where they would sleep that night.

And yet, when we asked Peter Paul how we could pray for them, he didn't even ask for prayer for himself. He asked that we pray for his parents. Their faith, he said, had been deeply shaken by seeing their son arrested and taken to jail. Could we pray that God would comfort and strengthen them?

His other request was for his ministry. He asked us to pray he would be able to continue as an evangelist—the very work that had just cost him a week in jail, his home, and the destruction of all he owned.

"Persecution is not an accident," he told us. "It is the expectation."

FOR REFLECTION

Maybe persecution is to be expected *in India*. Maybe it's the expectation when you're actively reaching Muslims for Christ. But what about us? Is persecution the expectation for comfortable free-world Christians? Or do we expect God will allow *us* only comfort, prosperity and earthly success? Jesus said, "If they persecuted me, they will also persecute you." Paul wrote to Timothy that "all who desire to live a godly life in Christ Jesus will be persecuted" (2 Tim. 3:12). I don't find an exception clause for any nationality.

For your journal: How does it change the way you think about faith and following Christ, if persecution is not an accident, but the expectation?

PRAYER

Jesus, help me to pray the same prayer Peter Paul prayed in prison: "Whatever is Your will, Lord, do it in my life." Whether Your will involves comfort or suffering, peace or heartache, health or disease. Whatever is Your will, Lord, do it in my life. Help me seek Your heart and sense Your presence in every circumstance.

For Your Journal

From My Journal

Sunday: We started out this morning interviewing a pastor who just got out of jail last night. We met his wife and two kids, too. He was amazingly cheerful and faithful!

Monday: I prayed for the pastor we met yesterday. And I thanked God for giving me a little window into what He is doing around the world. What an amazing privilege it is to do what I do—to see and meet His people; to hear their stories and see their faithfulness. It is truly my honor.

DAY 10

"WE PRAYED A LONG TIME..."

"Truly, truly, I say to you, unless a grain of wheat falls into the earth and dies, it remains alone; but if it dies, it bears much fruit."

JOHN 12:24

....

Tajikistan, 2004

There were still bullet holes in the window.

Sure, they'd put some tape over them. But it was hard not to notice they were there, and think about what they meant.

We sat in the front room of a home in Isfara, Tajikistan. The room also served as the meeting place for the city's only church (there were 126 mosques). It was also the room where the church's pastor, Sergei Bessarab, was shot through the window and killed just four months before our visit.

Sergei's widow, Tamara, sat with us. It was chilly, even though winter was supposed to have ended. She told us about her husband, the pastor of the church. Her grief and loss were still very close to the surface.

Before his death, Sergei Bessarab had been in prison five times, for eighteen of his forty-three years. But he wasn't imprisoned for Christ, or ministry activity. He was a criminal, a leading figure in Tajikistan's organized crime underworld. It was that life that led to long stays in prison.

But during his final imprisonment, everything changed. He met a Christian, a fellow prisoner who'd come to Christ through the prison ministry of the nation's Baptist churches. That friend, also named Sergei, began to pray that Jesus Christ, the Savior, would make Himself real to Sergei Bessarab.

Bessarab told his friend to stop praying for him. "Pray for someone else," he said. "Don't waste time praying for me."

Sergei didn't stop, though. He became the prisoner in charge of the prison chapel, and every day for three years he prayed his friend would come to know Christ. Finally, in August of 2000, his prayers were answered. Sergei Bessarab bent his knee, repented of his sin, and accepted Jesus as Savior and Lord.

The energy and passion he'd spent becoming a criminal leader were turned in a radical new direction. Six months after coming to faith, Bessarab was leading a prison Bible study. When he was released in 2001, he was baptized. And even after release from prison, he went back many times to visit, minister, and disciple prisoners. There were too many men inside those prisons—men he knew personally—who still needed to know Jesus.

Sergei Bessarab sensed God's call to plant a church in a city called Isfara. It was in the northwest part of the country, a city with zero Christian presence but a strong undercurrent of radical Islam. He and Tamara began to travel to Isfara on Sundays, holding services and ministering to people. Early in 2003, they moved there. The church began to grow, and the large front room of their home began to fill each Sunday. Sergei had a passion and charisma that drew people to hear his message, and after eighteen years in prison he knew that *nobody* was beyond the reach of God's grace.

The engine that powered Bessarab's public ministry was his private time with God. For two hours every morning and two more hours each evening, Sergei would sit in the front room—the room where the church met—and simply spend time with God. He would read his Bible, pray, and strum his guitar and sing songs of praise to the Father who rescued him from darkness and bondage.

But even with two hours in the morning and two hours at night, there was never enough time with Jesus. Tamara told us that, as 2003 came to a close, Sergei was praying for more time with the Lord: he was asking God to open up *two more hours*, in the middle of the day, that Sergei could spend in worship and prayer.

God answered Sergei Bessarab's prayer. But maybe not the way he expected.

Their little church—in a city where there had been no church—was getting noticed. Early in January, 2004, the local newspaper ran an article about the growing Christian church and their work turning Muslims into apostates. One line of the story stood out: "What's going to be done about Sergei Bessarab?"

Of course, Sergei read the article. But God had called him to Isfara, and he would wait to hear from God, not the local newspaper, as to when it was time to leave. He was sitting in the front room, guitar in his hand, softly singing songs of praise when the first shot rang out on January 12. In the quiet night, the gun sounded like a cannon. The glass of the front window spider webbed. The first shot hit Sergei in his strumming hand, spattering blood on the guitar. The second shot hit him in the leg. Hearing her husband cry out, Tamara got up from the back room of the house and rushed toward her husband.

The final shot hit Sergei in the chest. Tamara could do nothing more than watch her husband enter eternity. The gunman was still outside; he walked around the house firing indiscriminately. He also sprayed bullets into the Bessarabs' car, leaving it inoperable. Then he fled down an alley, disappearing into the dark night.

Now, four months later, we drove with Tamara to the cemetery where her husband's body had been laid. Tears streamed down her face as she leaned on the iron fence surrounding his grave. She'd been shattered by the murder.

"For twenty days, I could not take the Bible in my hands," she told us. "Then God started to show me His goodness."

She paused for a long moment, wiping the tears from her cheeks.

"The first time, I asked, 'Why, God? Why?' After that, I started to understand that it was God's plan. I began to study how to be thankful to God through this, and now I am thankful to God."

Her husband's headstone is inscribed with Philippians 1:21: "For to me to live is Christ, and to die is gain." Sergei had been asking God for two more hours each day to spend in His presence; now he would have not just two hours a day, but all of eternity!

Three bullets that January night couldn't end Bessarab's witness, and seeing the fruit of her husband's life and death was one part of God's comfort to Tamara. Even at the burial, Tamara saw fruit as her eighteen-year-old son, who had been running from Christ, committed his heart as he watched his stepfather's body lowered into the ground.

In only four months, Tamara had received letters from eight different prisons across Tajikistan from prisoners impacted by her husband's life and ministry.

But the impact wasn't contained by Tajikistan's borders.

"Many people have been awakened from spiritual sleep," said the Sergei, who had prayed for Bessarab to come to Christ. "Not only in Tajikistan, but also Kyrgyzstan and Kazakhstan. Many inmates in the prisons who heard his story came to know Christ more closely and wanted to commit their lives to Jesus." Bessarab walked with Jesus for less than four years, yet the fruit of that walk spread around the world.

Tamara also saw in her husband's death blessings for Isfara, the city God had called them to. "We prayed a long time that God would pay attention to Isfara," she said, "and now it's happened. God had His plan, and now He has turned the attention of many people [all over the world] to Isfara. God is preparing a special blessing. . . . We are asking God only one thing: to continue to have our ministry in the place where Sergei was killed. To continue his ministry."

There is one man, in particular, they hoped to reach. The son of a local mosque leader was arrested for Bessarab's murder. Sergei already had a plan for the young man who killed his friend, once he arrived in prison.

"One day, we will meet this person who killed Sergei, because we have a prison ministry all over Tajikistan. And we will be ready to tell him about Jesus."

FOR REFLECTION

There are many aspects of Sergei Bessarab's story that challenge us, but today focus on two of them. First, reflect on your personal time with God. Sergei was spending four hours a day in Scripture, prayer and worship—and *he didn't think it was enough*! He wanted *more* time with his heavenly Father. How is your time with God? Do you long for more time in His presence? What is the next step for you? Perhaps you need to begin having *daily* time with God. Perhaps, for you, a commitment to memorize God's Word or to more focused time in prayer. Write down *your next step*—and commit to take that step today.

Secondly, reflect on the challenge of the other Sergei. He prayed every day for *three years* for his friend to come to know Christ—even after Bessarab told him to stop wasting his time. If I've prayed for something every day for a week, I tend to think I've really persevered in my prayers! But three years? Every day? Who is God calling you to battle for in prayer, for as long as it takes? Write down their name and then set a daily reminder on your phone to pray.

PRAYER

"As a deer pants for flowing streams, so pants my soul for you, O God" (Ps. 42:1).

Jesus, give me a *longing* to be in Your presence, to learn from You and be shaped by You, a longing so strong that even four hours a day would seem too short a time to satisfy my need. Help me use my time well and wisely in order to grow the time I can spend in Your presence and Your Word.

And help me, Lord, endure in prayer, especially for those who don't know You yet. Let me never grow weary or bored or distracted from asking You to reveal Yourself to them.

For Your Journal

_____

_____

_____

_____

_____

_____

_____

_____

From My Journal

I heard today that four men from the village we'll visit tomorrow are currently incarcerated at Camp X-Ray in Guantanamo Bay. So it must be a Muslim fanatic hotbed!

[Members of Sergei's church] were encouraged by our presence. No other foreigners had visited the church—they came only to [a nearby city]. They fed us lunch (french fries, a potato/mushroom/onion mixture, bread—they have bread with everything here!) and tea, and we fellowshipped.

QUOTES TO CONSIDER

The same God allowed Stephen to be stoned and allowed Peter to escape from prison. God has been faithful, and His grace has been sufficient.

—Rose, the wife of a martyred pastor in northern Nigeria[2]

Blessed be the God and Father of our Lord Jesus Christ, the Father of mercies and God of all comfort, who comforts us in all our affliction, so that we may be able to comfort those who are in any affliction, with the comfort with which we ourselves are comforted by God. For as we share abundantly in Christ's sufferings, so through Christ we share abundantly in comfort too. If we are afflicted, it is for your comfort and salvation; and if we are comforted, it is for your comfort, which you experience when you patiently endure the same sufferings that we suffer. Our hope for you is unshaken, for we know that as you share in our sufferings, you will also share in our comfort.

For we do not want you to be unaware, brothers, of the affliction we experienced in Asia. For we were so utterly burdened beyond our strength that we despaired of life itself. Indeed, we felt that we had received the sentence of death. But that was to make us rely not on ourselves but on God who raises the dead. He delivered us from such a deadly peril, and he will deliver us. On him we have set our hope that he will deliver us again. You also must help us by prayer, so that many will give thanks on our behalf for the blessing granted us through the prayers of many.

2 Corinthians 1:3–11

DAY 11

FEAR IN ERITREA

Therefore, behold, I will allure her, and bring her into the wilderness, and speak tenderly to her.

HOSEA 2:14

....

Asmara, Eritrea, 2004

There have been two times in my international travels for VOM when I've been really scared. One of those times was a Monday night when I was scheduled to fly out of Eritrea.

Our hosts—pastors from banned evangelical churches in Asmara—had told my colleagues and me earlier that day that the police were asking about us. "Who are these foreigners? Why are they here?" It was our last day in the country; we would board our flight for home late that night.

During our time in Eritrea we'd heard firsthand accounts of persecution the church there had faced in the months since the government had called in evangelical church leaders and told them their churches could no longer hold public services. We'd interviewed Christians who'd been imprisoned in shipping containers or in hot desert camps. One man laid down on the floor to show us how he'd been bound in a pretzel-like position.

I'll never forget a woman we called Le'tay. During her mandatory military service another believer had led her to faith in Christ. Her faith brought her into a new spiritual family, and family members help each other. When seventy fellow Christians were arrested, Le'tay and another believer smuggled food and provisions to the prisoners. "How could I just keep quiet when my brothers were suffering?" she asked.

Their good deed was discovered, though, and they were punished. Determined to break Le'tay's faith, the government of President Isaias Afwerky—who is still in power as I write this—sent her to a prison in a hot desert location. They provided minimum food and maximum discomfort.

But what they thought would break her faith actually strengthened it.

"I have surrendered my life to Christ, so I did not have to be fearful," she explained.

She quoted Hosea 2:14: "I will lead her into the wilderness and speak tenderly to her." Le'tay talked about how that promise—made first to the wayward children of Israel—had come true in very personal ways for her during months in prison. She was in a wilderness, yes. But *God was there.* He spoke tenderly to her heart and spirit, encouraging and strengthening her each day.

"It was a good time," Le'tay told us of her six months in prison. She said the days went fast, because the Christians spent the time in worship together.

I'd heard these kinds of stories during our days in Eritrea. But I was fearful: I didn't want to experience an Eritrean prison. If the police had already been asking about us, they would likely have figured out we were booked on that night's flight. If they wanted to keep us, it would have to be before we got on that plane.

I was nervous on the drive to the airport. I was nervous handing my passport to the woman at the check-in counter. And really nervous when I went through immigration control. I didn't relax, even as we walked onto the tarmac and up the stairs into the plane. When they announced that the doors were closed, I began to relax. When the wheels left the ground, I breathed a sigh of relief. I would be making my trip home on schedule.

Only a few months later, I felt ashamed of my sense of relief that night. In widespread roundups across Eritrea, several church leaders we'd met with were arrested. Our friends were now in jail. Babies I'd held in my arms were now separated from fathers locked in prison.

It's been more than fifteen years since that night at the Asmara airport. As I write these words, some of my brothers are still in prison. I think of them often, and pray they are experiencing the same amazing ministry of the Holy Spirit Le'tay experienced; that they too will someday tell me being in prison was "a good time," and that the days went quickly.

If you are a follower of Christ, these families in Eritrea are *our family*. I hope you will say, like Le'tay did: "How can we just keep quiet and do nothing while our brothers and sisters are suffering for Jesus?"

Please pray for those we met who are still in prison in Eritrea. Pray they will know God's presence. Pray their physical needs will be met, their physical health protected. Pray they can witness to others, and see kingdom fruit for their time in prison.

I was afraid when we went to the airport that night. But twenty-some hours later, I was safely back home, hugging my family and thanking the Lord for a safe reunion. Pray with me that our brothers imprisoned in Eritrea will soon have a reunion with their families—a reunion almost two decades in the making.

FOR REFLECTION

What are you afraid of? What makes your stomach churn, or keeps you awake at night? On the day of his arrest, Pastor Richard Wurmbrand (the founder of The Voice of the Martyrs) recalled that the Bible has some variation of the command "Do not be afraid" 366 times—one for every day of the year, even if the year is a leap year. This was significant to Pastor Wurmbrand, because the date of his arrest was February 29.

Whatever today's date is, perhaps you need one of those 366 reminders. Find one of those "do not fear" verses and write it for your journal. Before this week is over, commit it to memory; say it out loud the next time you are afraid.

The God Who guides your path can be trusted. He has the power to bring good and blessing out of every situation, even being locked in a shipping container in an Eritrean desert. And because He's so trustworthy and powerful, you need not fear.

PRAYER

Dear Lord, help me never let fear keep me from doing Your will. Help me always pursue the path You lay before me. And Lord, please bless my brothers and sisters in Eritrea. Watch over those in prison. Protect them, care for them, and let them know Your amazing presence. Please let them know right now, supernaturally through Your Spirit, that they are being prayed for.

For Your Journal

_____

_____

_____

_____

_____

_____

_____

_____

From My Journal

We interviewed this morning a pastor who was arrested and beaten in 2002, then arrested and held for five days about a year ago. His story was an amazing one of God's faithfulness, and his spirit of love and humility was a blessing. He started out by making sure we knew that he hadn't been treated that badly, and that others had suffered way more than he had.

DAY 12

"IF GOD CAN USE US"

And I heard the voice of the Lord saying, "Whom shall I send, and who will go for us?" Then I said, "Here I am! Send me."
ISAIAH 6:8

∙∙

Southeast Asia, 2014

We met at a coffee shop on a bustling street in a Southeast Asian capital. When "Steve" and "Mai" walked in, they were what a fiction writer might call "nondescript." I'd call them regular people. But they are regular people that submitted their will to God's will, and He's taken their submission and allowed them to have an amazingly far-reaching ministry.

As Steve and Mai told their story, it was clear why my host in that country, who had introduced us, said, "They are just humble people."

Steve grew up in the United States. Mai was born in Southeast Asia, but her family fled the region during the Vietnam War (which, by the way, Vietnamese people call "The American War"). After two years in a refugee camp, when Mai and her family finally got on the plane to immigrate to America, she told herself, "I will *never* go back to Southeast Asia!" How God, Who sees the future as clearly as today, must've smiled when she said that! I've come to picture God nodding His head with a knowing smile when we try to tell Him what we'll never do.

Mai's family settled into the town where Steve was growing up. Steve and Mai were high school sweethearts, then husband and wife. They were hard-working, "regular" people. Steve owned a towing business. They raised their family and sought to build, with their lives, a Christian home.

After the children were raised and left home, Steve and Mai began to sense God calling them toward a ministry. The call was clear, but the details were not. They stepped out in faith, selling their home, selling the towing business, packing their bags, kissing their children and grandchildren goodbye and heading to Southeast Asia—the place Mai had promised herself she'd never go back to!

Their intention was to begin a ministry reaching out to girls wounded and scarred by the awful blight of human trafficking. They arrived in Southeast Asia and began taking steps toward such a work. But every step of the way they ran into roadblocks and obstacles. They couldn't seem to get the door to open even a crack!

Frustration and doubt crept in. Had they misheard God's call? Were they even supposed to have come to Asia? If God had called, why was He ignoring them now? What was the problem?

Slowly, God directed them to a new path. Mai's family is part of an ethnic group spread all across Southeast Asia, including many inside the closed nations of Vietnam, Laos, and China. God opened Steve and Mai's eyes to the needs among her tribal people for Christian teaching and music.

Steve decided to set up a little recording studio in their home. He went to YouTube and watched videos about audio recording equipment and editing software. Then he went on eBay and purchased some used studio equipment. When the equipment arrived, he set up a little studio in their home and Mai invited some friends from her tribal group in, and they began to record. Steve—who doesn't speak the tribal language—would edit the programs together, going back to YouTube or other online training sites when he ran into challenges.

The recordings were posted online, and also broadcast by the Far Eastern Broadcast Company—FEBC.

First, it was Bible teaching. Then they began to record Christian music in Mai's tribal language, the first time members of that people group had Christian songs in their heart language!

The people responded. Steve and Mai received emails from all over Asia—and even around the world—from people of Mai's tribal group blessed by their ministry. Some found Jesus for the first time; others had their faith strengthened to stand up to persecution and family pressure.

When radio professionals came to visit Steve and Mai, they looked at their studio with shock. "This is not right," one said, pointing out that you should never have the computer in the same room where the microphone is recording someone speaking or singing. A sensitive microphone will pick up the noise of the computer.

And yet, when they listened to the finished, edited programs, the audio quality was pristine, as if it'd been recorded in a million-dollar studio in Nashville or New York.

"How did you get this," one of the professionals asked, pointing to the earphones on his head, "from this?" He motioned to the makeshift studio in their home.

"I don't know," Steve told him. "I'm just a tow truck driver!"

As we sat in the coffee shop and I listened to them tell their story, what came from Steve and Mai was sheer wonder. They couldn't fathom how God would allow them—a tow truck driver and a housewife—to impact and bless people literally all over the world.

"Listen," Steve said near the end of our time together. "If God can use *us*, there's just *no limit* to what He can do!"

If God can use a woman that said she'd never go back to Southeast Asia to start a ministry in Southeast Asia . . . If God can use a tow truck driver who speaks only English to edit radio programs in a tribal language he doesn't even speak . . . If God can use a recording studio that was set up "all wrong" to produce pristine audio of people singing praise to Him in a language where such praises have never been recorded before . . .

"If God can use us, there's just *no limit* to what He can do!"

FOR REFLECTION

I've heard it said that "God doesn't call the qualified. He qualifies the called." If we are willing to surrender our lives, our comfort, our plans, and our security, then God is willing to use us in amazing ways to further His kingdom. David was a shepherd boy, the youngest of his family. Moses had a speech impediment. Peter was "just" a fisherman. And Steve was a tow truck driver.

Steve and Mai gave up a comfortable life in America to step out in faith. They moved thousands of miles from their children and grandchildren. They persevered when it seemed every path led straight into a brick wall. And now they're seeing the fruit God has brought from their humble willingness to serve wherever He asked.

Are you completely surrendered? Are you completely willing to go wherever God leads and do whatever He asks of you? If you're not, what is it that you can't let go of? Are you willing to ask God to *make* you willing? For your journal, write down the thing you struggle to lay down for the sake of Christ. When you are ready, write down, sign, and date your prayer of surrendering that thing to God.

PRAYER

"Here I am! Send me" (Isa. 6:8).

Lord, I am willing to go wherever You'd have me go, and do whatever You'd have me do. Help me see and eliminate any unwillingness in my life, so You can use me completely to do Your will.

For Your Journal

_____

_____

_____

_____

_____

_____

_____

_____

From My Journal

Today, the house [Mai] and [Steve] live in is only about a mile from the refugee camp where her family was held. He said they can walk there now, and tell by the fencing you see—even though it's now some kind of agricultural facility.

"You know, you put up a different kind of fence if you're trying to keep people out than if you're trying to keep animals in," he said.

I was really amazed and encouraged by their story.

They are just regular people that God called and they said yes. And now they are reaching people all over SE Asia via FEBC, and all over the world online. Glory!

Listen

Hear Steve and Mai tell their story on VOM Radio at www.VOMRadio.net/SteveMai

DAY 13

PATTERNS OF HOLINESS

Your word is a lamp to my feet and a light to my path.

PSALM 119:105

....

Hong Kong, 2015

John Short is, at least to me, a missionary legend. It's been more than fifty years since God called Short to His work for China. John got on a boat and went to Hong Kong, which at that time was as close as one could get to the tightly closed People's Republic. He worked to provide Christian literature to the Chinese church and to Christians in Hong Kong. When China cracked open its doors for visitors, John quickly applied for a visa. Since then, he's made scores of trips to all parts of the country. His work has resulted in thousands upon thousands of Bibles being placed into the hands of Chinese Christians.

Over time, God opened doors for John's ministry in other parts of Asia: Burma, Vietnam, even North Korea.

It was in 2013 that John visited North Korea. His trip took

longer than he'd planned, due to the fact that North Korean officials detained the then-73-year-old Australian. John was released 13 days later, after signing a forced confession that included his admission that "I wanted as many North Koreans to become Christians as possible." Amen!

After his release, John granted only two interviews: one with his hometown paper back in Australia, and the other with me for broadcast on VOM Radio.

I flew to Hong Kong. The next day, I went to the Christian Book Room, the ministry John has led for so many decades. I arrived in time for the daily devotion for all the staff. They sat around a table and read through a Bible passage, each one reading a verse. The Bible was the center of the conversation. Then we prayed.

After the devotional, I joined the staff for lunch; and later that afternoon, I sat down with John. The following day, I would interview his wife, Karen, too, to hear her side of the saga while John was detained, being in Hong Kong and dealing with nosy journalists and even North Korean spies.

John said when he arrived in North Korea, they carefully went through his suitcase. Right on the top, as it is for every trip John takes, was his Bible.

"I make a point of putting my Bible on the top, my personal Bible, on the top of my possessions," John explained. "Before each entrance [to North Korea] our possessions are investigated. If a North Korean says, 'What's that?' I say, 'That's a Bible, my Bible.'

"They say, 'You can't take that into North Korea.' I say, 'If I can't take that in, I don't go in; then you will have to cancel my visit because I am a Christian, I read my Bible every day, I need this with me.'

"Then they will call in others and have a little debate about it and say, 'We shouldn't let you carry it.' I say, 'I need it, I have to have it.'

I feel it is a testimony to them in this. Then they will say, 'It will be recorded, you must bring this out again.' I say, 'It's an English Bible. I don't think Koreans would enjoy it as much as I do. It is my Bible. I give you my word I will bring it out again.'"

John didn't know it when he entered North Korea that time, but having his Bible with him would make a huge difference.

John was part of a tour group, and one of the sites they visited was a Buddhist temple. Yet when they arrived to see the temple, it'd been vandalized. The North Korean tour guides, whose entire job is showing foreigners how wonderful life in North Korea is, were horribly embarrassed. They rushed around, trying to survey the damage and figure out whether it was something they could fix quickly and get on with the tour, or whether it was too embarrassing to The Dear Leader and whether they should take the foreigners elsewhere. It's hard for us to imagine, but those guides' freedom and maybe even their lives could depend on how they responded in that situation.

Taking advantage of the confusion, John surreptitiously tucked some gospel tracts outside the temple, in a place he hoped they'd be found after he left. He'd had the tract translated into Korean and printed, then secretly stashed copies in his suitcase.

The next morning, John packed his bags for the flight from Pyongyang back to Beijing. When he approached the car for the ride to the airport, however, he was told that he would not be making the flight. The tracts had been found, and John had a lot of explaining to do. Thus began days of morning-and-afternoon interrogations. The questions started with the tracts: Who translated them? Where were they printed? But soon, they delved into John's entire life. He was asked to write out, year by year, literally every event of his life. And the North Koreans checked up on him. He found out later they'd sent agents to his office in Hong Kong and even to his boyhood home in Australia.

This wasn't John's first time to be detained or interrogated, and he'd certainly thought through the price he was willing to pay to answer God's call. He told me in his bold, Australian-accented voice about persecution, and how great saints of the Chinese church he'd known and worked alongside influenced his thoughts on the matter. Many of them had spent not weeks but decades in prison. One of the quotes I remember well was this gem: "Fear and faith cannot exist within my heart at the same time. When we live by faith, trusting the Lord moment by moment, fear has no room in the heart."

The questioning continued. But John still had his Bible, and he'd established long ago that the words of that Book were the foundation of his life. He and Karen also had a pattern of reading. For all of their married life, they'd read the Bible each day. In addition to other readings, they read a chapter from Proverbs and a chapter from John's gospel each day. On the first day of the month, they read the first chapter of those books. On the second day of the month, the second chapters, and so on.

John was not allowed to have any contact with the outside world during his detention. He couldn't call his wife and tell her he was okay. But he told me—several months after his release, after life had calmed somewhat—that reading those chapters each day, and knowing she was reading the same words, gave him a sense of spiritual connection greater than any phone line could ever offer.

The next day, I interviewed Karen. I had done a phone interview with her while John was detained. Now we sat across the table from each other in her home. Her Australian accent carried calm, thoughtful answers to my questions. In the years she and John had been involved in China ministry, it wasn't uncommon for him to be detained. Karen was used to praying for him without knowing exactly what he might be facing when she prayed.

"My request for John," she told me, "only one thing I asked [the

Lord] really, was that he would be able to keep his Bible. I thought, 'If he has the Word of God with him, he will be fine if he can read the Scriptures.' Thankfully, God answered that prayer."

She didn't have to wonder what he'd be reading.

"A daily habit, we read a certain chapter, certain books [of the Bible] every day, plus other things. I thought if he had the Scriptures we would be on the same page."

Through thirteen days, in spite of zero communication with each other, John and Karen were very much on the same page. And when the call came from John, asking her to come to Beijing and "fetch" him, she was thankful for God's answer to her prayers for John to return home safely. But she wasn't closed to him going back to North Korea at some point in the future.

In fact, she said that if the Lord opened the door, she'd like to go with him!

FOR REFLECTION

I was challenged by John and Karen's story, and by the absolute priority they place on the Scriptures in their lives and their marriage. Are you that serious about God's Word? Is time in the Word such a pattern in your life that others can look at the calendar and know what you're reading? Or look at the clock and know, "Oh, it's 6 in the morning. They're in the Word right now"? Reading God's Word is changing me from the inside out. And it can change you too. But, like John and Karen Short, you must make it a pattern of holiness, an anchor point in your daily life.

Make the decision to read God's Word each day, and set up a plan. Perhaps start, as John and Karen do, with each day's chapter of John and Proverbs. Perhaps you'll use a print Bible, or maybe an app on your phone. For your journal, find and read Scriptures about God's Word (you can start with Hebrews 4:12; Psalm 119; 2

Timothy 3:16–17; and Isaiah 40:8. There are lots of others!), then write down ways you can put those verses into practice.

PRAYER

Lord, give me a love for Your Word! Help me to long for it each day. Help me hear Your voice when I open the pages of Scripture, and to be changed as I read, shaped more each day into a reflection of Your Son, Jesus.

For Your Journal

_____

_____

_____

_____

_____

_____

_____

_____

_____

_____

From My Journal

The first time I met Mr. Short was in November of 1999. My coworkers and I were on our way to China, but stopped in Hong Kong on the way. We happened to be here on a Sunday morning, and went to Mr. Short's church. I remember that afternoon he took us for "afternoon tea" at the super-ritzy Peninsula Hotel in Hong Kong. He said a room there was $350 per night, and I remember I ordered iced tea (which I now know is not common in Asia), and that there were no free refills. So I sat through a lot of our conversation with an empty glass in front of me wishing that other countries would pick up on America's free refill idea!

He was already a missions hero then, having worked decades in China. But I couldn't have imagined then that he would someday wind up detained inside North Korea.

Listen

You can hear my interviews with John and Karen Short at www.VOMRadio.net/short.

PRAYING FOR PERSECUTED CHRISTIANS

Sometimes it's harder to see someone we love suffer than it would be to suffer ourselves.

The spouses and children of persecuted Christians endure this kind of suffering, as well as suffering that comes when their own lives and livelihoods are affected by having their family member in prison.

PRAY TODAY for the spouses and children of imprisoned Christians. Pray God will encourage and give them strength, and will provide for their physical and spiritual needs.

Pray for marriages impacted by forced separations, that God will intertwine husband and wife spiritually through His presence and His Word.

Pray children will not grow disenchanted or bitter towards God because of their parents' imprisonment, but will carry on a legacy of faithful kingdom service for which their parents are willing to suffer.

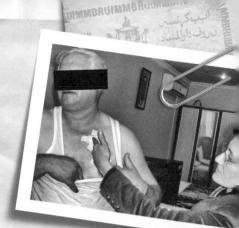

DAY 14

BULLET HOLES IN YOUR COAT

> "My God sent his angel and shut the lions' mouths, and they have not harmed me, because I was found blameless before him; and also before you, O king, I have done no harm."

DANIEL 6:22

....

Northern Iraq, 2008

Pastor Hakim was one of the few remaining Protestant pastors in Mosul amidst the chaos of war-torn Iraq in 2008. When we met him, he told us that his church had a staff of three pastors two years earlier. One of the pastors was killed by Sunni radicals. The other moved to Europe for his and his family's safety. But Hakim stayed on to shepherd his flock in Mosul.

Eight days before our meeting, Hakim had been met, when he pulled into the parking lot where he worked, by three men with guns. They'd been sent specifically to kill *the pastor*, and Hakim later learned they'd been asking about him. "Where is the Christian?" they'd demanded from others nearby.

The three men with guns ordered Hakim to stop the car. But he knew stopping the car meant almost-certain death. He immediately put the car in reverse and backed away, but not before he was hit three times with bullets. At the hospital, Muslim doctors asked him what he was doing with his life.

"The way the bullets went in you [missing organs and major blood vessels]," the doctors said, "this is a miracle."

It was only eight days after the shooting when Hakim came to another city to meet with my colleague and me. His wounds were still bandaged. And he still wore the coat he'd worn that morning. He put his finger through one of the bullet holes, just to the side of one of the buttons that ran up the front of the coat. He took off his shirt, to show us the still-bandaged wounds, two X's of bandages on the left side of his chest.

I couldn't understand how there could be a bullet hole in his coat and two bullet holes in his chest and Hakim still be alive and walking around. "These are my medals," he said, pointing at the bandages, and to the scars beneath. It was true that he was the victor in a great spiritual battle. But his "medals" weren't the kind any Christian wants to "win."

Hakim and his wife, "Nadira," shared the story of their ministry. God had called them to the church in Mosul, and in spite of chaos and violence and death around them, they didn't feel He'd called them to leave yet. So they stayed.

The pressure was intense. Pressure from Sunni radicals who wanted to force every Christian in the city to accept Islam—or leave. They would call Hakim to tell him why he should choose to follow Muhammad, and what would happen to him and his family if he didn't.

There was pressure also from their relatives, who had relocated to safety in Europe. "Come out of there," they would say every single week during their phone calls. "Come to a safe place. We're ready to welcome you and take care of you when you arrive."

Hakim and Nadira had daughters in the university in Mosul, facing danger every single day as they pursued their education. The year before, a Christian woman had been killed for distributing Bibles. Every member of their family knew the risks of living as a Christian in Mosul. Their lives were in danger. Yet they stayed. For God hadn't told them to leave.

Every week they told their relatives in Europe, "God has called us to Mosul. We are staying."

Nadira told us in accented English how God had been ministering to her, even in the days right before the shooting of her husband. She'd sensed His presence in very real ways. She sensed His hand strengthening her, injecting and molding the steel in her spine she would need in the hours and days after her husband was shot.

FOR REFLECTION

As I think about Nadira and Hakim and their story, I think of two things. The first is God's ability to protect the things and the people He has placed. Hakim was shot three times, including twice in the chest—and was walking around talking about it eight days later! If God wants you to survive something—no matter how dire or threatening it is—you will survive.

The second thought I have is about answering God's call, and keeping on answering until He issues a different call. How often, when the road becomes rocky and rough, do we look for a different, easier road? But sometimes God has great learning, and even great blessings, along our most difficult roads.

If today you are walking a difficult road, write down the things you're learning and ways you see God working or teaching you. If you are on a comfortable, easy road at this moment, write a prayer of thanksgiving for the season of rest and ease.

PRAYER

Lord Jesus, thank You for Your amazing power to protect and sustain those You've called to Your service. Help me answer Your call, and keep answering each day and each moment until You call me somewhere else here on earth or call me to the "better country" that will be my eternal home.

For Your Journal

_____

_____

_____

_____

_____

_____

_____

_____

_____

From an Email I Sent Char That Night

We just had THE BOMB interview . . . absolutely THE BOMB! Pastor from Mosul shot three times LAST SUNDAY (the day after your birthday). And he was here in our rooms, interviewing with us, along with his wife. And he shows us the bandages over the entry and exit wounds. AND HE'S STILL WEARING THE SAME COAT . . . WITH THE BULLET HOLES IN IT! (Can you tell this gets me a little jazzed up?)

And he points to the wounds, and he says "These are my medals (like military medals)." And his wife said that the night before he was shot she was listening to Christian music and the Lord really came and ministered to her . . . like she could feel His presence really close. And then she went to bed, and the next morning her husband was shot. She reminded me of Sabina Wurmbrand. Said that she would never urge her husband to leave, because God had called him there to the work.

They've been told by ALL their family members to leave Mosul. That it's not safe. That they have daughters and should go. But they say they are staying there because Jesus called them there. He is the only evangelical pastor left in a city of two million people!

Amazing, amazing, amazing testimony! Worth the trip!

DAY 15

A TESTIMONY IN THE GROUND

> Do not be deceived: God is not mocked, for whatever one sows, that will he also reap. For the one who sows to his own flesh will from the flesh reap corruption, but the one who sows to the Spirit will from the Spirit reap eternal life. And let us not grow weary of doing good, for in due season we will reap, if we do not give up.
>
> **GALATIANS 6:7–9**

. . . .

Nepal, 2012

Nepal is one of the most beautiful places I've ever been. In one of the cities we visited, I could step out of my hotel room, and if the day was clear I could see four of the world's ten tallest mountains, just looking from the balcony outside my room. When you're flying, and you look out the airplane window and have to look UP to see the tops of the mountains—wow!

It was in Nepal where I met Pastor Salindra, a man willing to take a beating over a member of his congregation who was already dead!

When a Christian brother we'll call "Bilal" died in a small Nepali city, it was important to his family that his body be buried. It's hard for many American Christians to understand the priority our Nepali family members place on this ritual, but in their culture a burial and a tombstone is not just a way to dispose of a body but an "Ebenezer" (1 Sam. 7:12)—a permanent landmark of a person's faith and God's faithfulness.

In Bilal's city, there are about thirty thousand people, but at that time, there were only four or five Christian families. When he died, radical Hindus came to get his body for cremation, according to Hindu custom. Bilal's family said no, they wanted a Christian funeral and burial instead.

Pastor Salindra, the young pastor who leads their church, was at their home to help with funeral arrangements when he heard shouting outside the house. A large Hindu mob had gathered. The people were shouting and threatening: they *demanded* the body be given to them in order to perform Hindu last rights and cremation.

As he told me the story, Salindra explained that in the life of a Hindu, there are three significant milestones: birth, marriage, and death. By cremating Bilal's body, the Hindus hoped to erase his Christian testimony. Cremation would be a message to everyone that he hadn't *really* been a Christian; that in his final moments he'd rejected the "foreign" religion of Christianity and returned to Hinduism. A grave, in contrast, would be a permanent testimony that this man who had died was *a Christian*. Why else would his body be buried instead of cremated according to Hindu custom?

Salindra stepped outside of the house and told the Hindus that Bilal was a Christian and the family wanted a Christian funeral. The mob became enraged, grabbing Salindra and two other Christians and beating them with sticks and clenched fists. The three Christians ran for their lives, trying to get on their bicycles and get out of the area. But the mob continued to attack.

The Christians found refuge in the home of Bimala, an aged Christian widow who opened her door to the fleeing Christians, motioning them inside in spite of the angry mob coming after them. Why would she invite attacks on her home by sheltering the Christians?

"I am the Lord's servant," she told us, "so I have to be strong. I will not fear, because He is with us. I thought that some of those people might make problems for me, but I have to be strong."

The mob of angry Hindus backed off, and Christians were able to come on motorbikes and whisk Salindra and the others in the house out of danger. Salindra was treated for wounds received in the beating. His body was well, but in his heart there was a struggle. For a week after the attack, he couldn't sleep.

"I was praying for myself and I understood, when reading the Bible, that I have to forgive [the Hindus who attacked me], because the Lord says if you don't forgive others, you will not be forgiven. Those words were pricking my heart."

God continued to draw Salindra to forgive his attackers by reminding him of the forgiveness he had received.

"I have also done some wrong things, some mistakes, so the Lord is working. [He forgave me.] So I have to forgive. The Lord was speaking to me, 'Forgive them. They have to come to Me.' The Lord was speaking to me. Then I said yes. I have to work with them so they will come to Christ." A month after the attack, Salindra came to the point of fully forgiving those who'd attacked and injured him.

He continued to minister in that city, even though after the attacks his congregation shrunk by half. Many Christians shrank back in fear. They didn't want to risk becoming targets of radical Hindus by going to the church or gathering with other Christians. For those that continued to attend church, Salindra began a series of sermons to enable and encourage them to withstand persecution he knows they'll face.

"One day, everyone has to die," he tells his congregation. "The life here [on earth] is very short. Whatever they do to us because we're Christian—what we will go through—even if we have to die, we'll die because we'll have a long life [in eternity with Christ]."

Believers too fearful to come to church sometimes asked Salindra to come to their homes and pray with them. They weren't willing to publicly be identified as Christians, but they still wanted to quietly meet with their pastor for encouragement and prayer. Salindra has faith that, one day, their courage will be strengthened and they will return to meeting with the church. "I believe they will come one day," he says, "because they have tasted the Lord."

And, for all time, there is a grave marker witnessing that there *are* Christians in that city. Bilal's family, for generations to come, can go to his grave and remember his faith. "See! Our father was a Christian! If he'd been a Hindu, he would have been cremated. There would be no grave, no marker of his life. But he was a Christian!" The mark of his faith is right there in the ground.

FOR REFLECTION

Western cultures have very different ideas about death. We don't think of a tombstone as a testimony like our Christian family in Nepal does. But all of us *are* leaving a testimony. All of us, with our lives, are leaving signs for our families, our churches, and unbelievers around us. What signs are you leaving? What will people say after you're gone into eternity? Will they say, "That was a Christian!" Or will there be doubts? Write ten words that describe the kind of spiritual legacy you want to leave for your family and friends, and then live today in such a way as to leave clear signs of your faith in Christ.

PRAYER

Lord, Creator of the universe, unbound by time, help me live today in a way that my life will leave godly marks for eternity on those around me. Empower me to live in such a way that, after I die, my family, coworkers, and friends will be able to say, without hesitation, "He was a Christian!" or "She was a Christian!"

For Your Journal

_____

_____

_____

_____

_____

_____

_____

_____

_____

_____

From My Journal

[We met] a pastor whose life is constantly threatened [because of his gospel work]. He failed the eighth grade, yet he leads a church that has birthed fourteen daughter churches! A very faithful brother and worker! It was funny when we finished talking to him. He said he didn't want to walk out with us, because if his landlord saw him with Westerners, then the landlord would raise his rent!

QUOTES TO CONSIDER

As Elisabeth Elliot points out, not even dying a martyr's death is classified as extraordinary obedience when you are following a Savior who died on a cross. Suddenly a martyr's death seems like normal obedience.

—David Platt[3]

Not only that, but we rejoice in our sufferings, knowing that suffering produces endurance, and endurance produces character, and character produces hope, and hope does not put us to shame, because God's love has been poured into our hearts through the Holy Spirit who has been given to us.

Romans 5:3–5

DAY 16

"THAT WAS A WONDERFUL TIME"

> Then King Nebuchadnezzar was astonished and rose up in haste. He declared to his counselors, "Did we not cast *three* men bound into the fire?" They answered and said to the king, "True, O king." He answered and said, "But I see *four* men unbound, walking in the midst of the fire, and they are not hurt; and the appearance of the fourth is like a son of the gods."
>
> **DANIEL 3:24–25**

....

China, 2002

It was my second VOM visit to China. I was able to take my wife along—her first overseas trip and a window for her into the work and travel I do for VOM. We first went to Vietnam, where we interviewed persecuted Christians from the Hmong tribal group while driving around in the back of a van—there wasn't any place they felt safe being seen with Westerners.

After our time in Vietnam, we went to China, where we met Sister Tong. She'd been released from prison a few weeks before our arrival. I was to interview her, then write a story about her witness and her time in prison.

Sister Tong hosted an unregistered church meeting in her home in China. Churches there are required to register with the government and come under control of the Communist Party's "Religious Affairs" officials. A church that registers is told when and where they're allowed to meet, and who is allowed to lead those meetings. Children under eighteen aren't supposed to attend. All religious activities are expected to take place only as approved by the government.

Any gathering of Christians outside this system and without government approval is an "illegal religious gathering." Those caught at such meetings are subject to interrogation, arrest, and detention. But as a practical matter at that time, Public Security Bureau officers focused mostly on hosts and leaders, rather than trying to arrest every single person caught attending.

So Sister Tong, who hosted such a gathering in her home, was arrested and sent to prison for six months. It was an effort by the government to "re-educate" her to think more like a Communist and less like a person who has put on "the mind of Christ" (1 Cor. 2:16).

Sister Tong came to meet with us at a location where we could have some privacy; it would certainly create even more trouble for her if she was caught meeting foreigners. She was small, with tiny shoulders. My wife, who is five feet seven inches tall, seemed to tower over Sister Tong. We greeted her and exchanged pleasantries and small talk through our translator. Then I got out my recorder to begin the interview.

First question: "So tell me about the prison."

I was thinking we'd set the stage for her story by diving right in to her suffering. I expected to hear colorful details about how difficult prison life was: the bed was so hard, the food was so terrible, the rats were so big! I waited expectantly as the translator turned my question from English into Mandarin. The recorder was running; my pen was ready to capture every detail of the picture she would paint with her words.

When Sister Tong heard my question from the translator, her face lit up with what I can only call a heavenly smile. She said something to the translator in Chinese. He turned to us.

"Oh yes. That was a *wonderful* time."

I turned to the translator. Now I was confused. I'd asked about *prison*, and Sister Tong got this huge smile on her face and said it was wonderful. My translator must not have understood my question. Something had misconnected, hadn't it? Because, in my understanding, there was no way anyone would ever say that prison was wonderful. Right?

Or was there?

The translator assured me that he had translated my question— and her answer—accurately. "Oh yes. That was a *wonderful* time."

I definitely had more questions for Sister Tong now. How could prison be wonderful? What was it about the experience that would bring such a smile to her face when she thinks back on it?

She was only too happy to answer.

Prison was wonderful because God was there with her! Sister Tong shared how close, how special, her relationship with Jesus had been in prison. It was like He paid extra attention to her during that time and her heart was warmed daily by His exceptional presence and touch. She felt so close to the Creator of the universe in prison that it was hard to think of that time as anything other than wonderful.

And it wasn't just Christ's presence; He'd also allowed Sister Tong an amazing ministry in prison. She'd had the opportunity to lead several cellmates into a relationship with Christ. What could be more wonderful than seeing someone snatched from the kingdom of hell and brought into the eternal kingdom of Jesus Christ?

Oh, yes. That was a wonderful time.

Sister Tong didn't really care to talk about the physical conditions inside the prison; she was much more focused on the spiritual conditions. And for her the spiritual conditions had been wonderful!

My conversation with Sister Tong changed me. It changed my mind in some profound ways.

Before that conversation, I really didn't have a frame of reference that could even consider going to prison as something wonderful. You see, going to prison was *suffering*, and suffering is to be avoided if there is any possible way to avoid it, right? But Sister Tong hadn't avoided suffering, and in fact when she thought back on it now she got this amazing smile on her face, as if she'd just peeked through the keyhole into heaven.

If prison wasn't suffering, but was instead a wonderful time, what else might I be missing? What else might be wonderful if it was given to us out of the hand of a loving Savior? Could sickness be wonderful? Could unemployment be wonderful? Could financial loss be wonderful?

What if those things led to experiencing the closeness of Christ in a new and powerful way? What if those things led us to know Jesus more, and to give more of ourselves to Him? What if those experiences opened doors of ministry in a new way, and allowed us to reach with the gospel people we otherwise would never have encountered? Was there anything that couldn't be wonderful if it was being used by God?

The translator didn't mess up the question, or the answer. But Sister Tong messed with my mind that day. She changed the way I think about prison and suffering. She opened my eyes to the fact that even the "worst" places on earth could be places of blessing and God's presence. They truly could be *wonderful.*

FOR REFLECTION

Is there some situation in your life right now that is not what you hoped or expected? Is it two or three miles (or more) from what you'd think of as *wonderful*? Is it possible in that circumstance God may be moving? Is it possible in that situation you might experience Him in a new, special way? Or perhaps He's put you in a setting where you'll have contact with someone you'd otherwise never meet—someone who doesn't yet know about Jesus' love for them. Are you willing to see that situation—which you may have never wanted or expected— as *wonderful*? For your journal, write about those circumstances and how you see God at work in the midst of them.

PRAYER

Lord God, thank You that, with You, even a prison cell can be *wonderful*. I bring my challenging situation with _____ to You. Your Word tells me to "Rejoice in the Lord always" (Phil. 4:4), and so right now, I choose to rejoice in spite of my circumstances. I ask that, like Sister Tong, I can experience a special closeness with Jesus, even in a setting I didn't want or plan to be in. Please give me spiritual eyes to see the needs of those around me, and a willingness to speak Your name and Your love to those I encounter. Amen.

For Your Journal

_____

_____

_____

_____

_____

_____

_____

_____

_____

From My Journal

We're struggling a little bit to get these dear folks to talk about the hardships they've faced. They honestly don't even think about it! It's like pulling teeth to get them to describe an arrest or a prison cell.

DAY 17

"HE JUST LOVES GOD MORE NOW"

Then our mouth was filled with laughter, and our tongue with shouts of joy; then they said among the nations, "The LORD has done great things for them." The LORD has done great things for us; we are glad.

PSALM 126:2–3

....

Prague, Czech Republic, 2017

It is one thing to go to meet someone who has endured persecution. It's quite another thing when you're going to meet someone *you already know well*, right after they've gone through a season of intense persecution. That's what made this trip different. In some ways, there were more question marks than on a "regular" VOM trip.

I was to go and interview Petr Jasek only eight days after he was released from fourteen months in prison in Sudan. He'd been tried as a spy and sentenced to "life" in prison—which in Sudanese law means 20 years—plus four extra years. Thankfully, the Czech government had negotiated his release and he was now back home.

I wasn't going to *meet* Petr. We'd been coworkers for more than a decade, and had traveled together into other persecuted countries. He had been in our home, and my family had been in his. But that was *before* fourteen months in prison, including time sharing a cell with ISIS fighters who'd also been arrested in Sudan. Who knew how different the Petr we met in Prague would be from the old Petr? We had consulted experts about what to expect, and how to help Petr process the experience and suffering that he'd endured. What if he'd endured torture? What if his mind or his body had been damaged? What would he need from us? How long might he bear the scars of those long incarcerated months?

My flight arrived in Prague in the late afternoon, and we were to meet Petr and his family for dinner. I showered quickly and came down to the lobby of the hotel at the appointed time, and there was Petr. He was skinnier, yes, but smiling broadly. What an honor to hug him and tell him welcome home, and how we and so many others had been praying for him.

We spent large chunks of the next four days in a room together as Petr recounted the story from beginning to end. He started with the moment he'd gone to the airport to fly out of Sudan, only to have two security officers tap him on the shoulder after he'd gotten his boarding pass. And he finished on the day he was sitting outside reading from the Psalms when a prison guard at Kober Prison came to tell him, "Petr, you're being released."

There were so many amazing parts to Petr's story. Almost being waterboarded by his ISIS cellmates. Being put in solitary confinement, and considering it a blessing. The way he was able to talk by phone to his family regularly from inside of prison.

The part of his story I found most amazing was the way God had prepared him. Certainly, Petr's life had prepared him. From growing up in the home of a persecuted pastor in a Communist country to traveling the world to meet with and interview persecuted Christians, Petr's persecution education had been long and intense. But even more than that, God had prepared him in a unique way: a dream.

Two years before Petr's trip to Sudan, he'd had a dream one night in which he clearly saw himself in a prison cell. He clearly saw the cell door close, and heard the click of the lock, and in his dream he understood this wasn't to be a short stay in prison. The dream was so real, so profound, that Petr looked disturbed when he arrived at church the next morning. So disturbed a Christian friend asked, "Petr, what's wrong?"

More than two years later, on the night Petr was arrested in Sudan, he was interrogated for about 24 hours before finally being taken to a cell at the National Intelligence and Security Service (NISS) headquarters. The cell was intended for a single prisoner, but there were already six men inside: one on the bed, and five more on the floor. Those on the floor began to scoot together to make room for Petr to lay down.

Petr was ushered inside by one of the NISS guards, and when he turned back to watch the door close to lock him inside, he was immediately taken back to the night of his dream. It was the *exact same door* he'd seen in the dream. The same color. The same small window in the middle of it. The same clicking sound as it locked shut. And Petr knew God had been preparing him for this cell, even two years before.

That was the first of many jaw-dropping moments in Petr's story. I'm still in awe that he spent fourteen months in prison in Sudan without getting malaria. I'd been in Sudan for *six days* and came home with that awful disease!

Petr talked about the day, four months into his imprisonment, when he'd led some fellow prisoners to faith in Christ. He'd been frustrated and anxious before that, asking God how long he would have to stay in prison. But after that day—and seeing that God was allowing him to have an eternal impact in prison—his attitude completely changed. His prayer went from "how long?" to "As long as You want me here, and as long as You'll give me a ministry here, I'll stay."

He talked about how thirsty he was for God's Word when he was finally allowed a Bible in prison. The only way he had enough light to read it was to stand by the window of his cell, so he stood from the morning until dinner time, hungrily feasting on Scripture. He read the whole Bible in three weeks!

The ministry God allowed Petr only grew from there. He was transferred to a different prison with a prison chapel and he was able to preach to hundreds of fellow prisoners. And he was ready, because the hours and hours he had spent soaking in God's Word gave him plenty to preach about.

By the end of our time together in Prague, I was amazed at how God had uniquely prepared Petr—and his wife and children—for his ordeal, and also sustained and shepherded him through it.

When I arrived home, Char asked me how Petr was. For months, we had prayed together for him, and both of us wondered what suffering he'd endured, and how it might affect him.

"It's amazing," I told her. "He's the very same Petr. He just loves God more now."

FOR REFLECTION

One of the things Petr shared was the difference the prayers of God's people made for him in prison. He was always amazed that he would lay down at nine each night, when the lights went out in the prison, and immediately go to sleep. When he arrived home, he discovered that the people of his church had made a commitment that every night at eight, they would stop what they were doing and pray for Petr; for his safety, his encouragement, and his health. Suddenly, Petr understood his restful sleep: eight in the Czech Republic is nine in Sudan. His ability to go right to sleep every night—no matter what was going on around him—was a direct result of people praying for him right at that time! Make a commitment to pray each day for Christians, like Petr, in prison for their faith in Christ. You can find their names and stories (and write them letters) at www.PrisonerAlert.com. Perhaps set a reminder on your phone, or place their picture by your Bible or on your refrigerator. But choose to pray every day, and remember from Petr's story what a difference your prayers make.

PRAYER

Lord, help me never discount the power of prayer in my life, or in the lives of those I'm praying for. Thank You that You have prepared us and You will empower us for whatever we face this day. Help me walk forward boldly with confidence in You. And may the challenges I face lead me, like they did Petr, to love You more.

For Your Journal

_____

_____

_____

_____

From My Journal

I had conversations before Petr's release about what he'd be like after fourteen months in prison. How would it have affected him? What damage to his body and mind would be evident after harsh prison conditions? I'm happy to report that there is no "damage" to Petr. He is the same Petr . . . he just loves God MORE than ever before! It was really remarkable to be with him.

Listen

You can hear my conversations with Petr, recorded in Prague, at www.VOMRadio.net/Petr.

PRAY FOR PERSECUTED CHRISTIANS

One thing I like to pray for our persecuted family members is that God will let them know, through His Spirit, that they are being prayed for.

Petr found out after he got home from Sudan that people were praying every night at the time he was going to bed.

But I've also heard how God answers that prayer more immediately. I asked Gracia Burnham, a missionary and former hostage in the Philippines, about the people who prayed for her and her husband, Martin, when they were held hostage by a radical Muslim group.

She said that, at different points during their long months in captivity, Martin would look at her and say, "Someone is praying for us right now." At other times, she would tell him the same. Somehow, they knew!

PRAY TODAY that Christians enduring persecution will know—even in the moments you are praying!—that they are not forgotten and are being prayed for right at this very moment.

DAY 18

JOY IN GOD'S PLAN

Now the word of the LORD came to Jonah the son of Amittai, saying, "Arise, go to Nineveh, that great city, and call out against it, for their evil has come up before me." But Jonah rose to flee to Tarshish from the presence of the LORD. He went down to Joppa and found a ship going to Tarshish. So he paid the fare and went down into it, to go with them to Tarshish, away from the presence of the LORD.

JONAH 1:1–3

....

Jordan, 2016

Pastor Aqil leads an evangelical church in Jordan. The country, like much of the Middle East, is almost 100 percent Muslim. Aqil's church is not illegal, but it's certainly not popular. Threats and pressure against their work—especially any kind of outreach to Muslims—is not uncommon.

After the civil war heated up next door in Syria, destroying that nation from the inside, tens of thousands of refugees streamed into Aqil's native Jordan. Aqil was aware of their arrival, and vaguely aware of their terrible struggle to eke out a life in his country. But he already had a ministry: he was leading a church. He already faced pressure and persecution.

Then a donor called the church, offering funding to help Aqil reach out with aid to Syrian refugees. Politely, Aqil told the donor, "No, thank you." His task list was full. He wasn't looking to start new ministries, or for more ways to fill up his weekly calendar.

But he felt, very clearly, God telling him not to close his heart to the refugees or to this ministry opportunity. After a night of not sleeping well, arguing with God, Aqil called back the donor. Yes, he said, he would be willing to help deliver aid if the donor's offer was still available.

And so began a ministry. Aqil and others from his church began traveling to an area where thousands of refugees lived in makeshift shelters, tents, or whatever they could find. They had no way of supporting themselves. Their children were not welcome in local schools.

The refugees came from many different faith streams. Some were nominal Christians, some Yazidi, some Shia, some Sunni. All were desperate. All were far from home.

In addition to offering humanitarian aid, Aqil and the Christians from his church would offer prayer. And they made clear, every time, that they would be praying to Jesus—*Isa al Masih*—not to Allah or Muhammed. It was very rare that anyone would turn down their offer of prayers. The refugees, after all, were desperate for help; what could it hurt to ask Jesus, too?

One day, they were in the home of a woman and her children, and again the pastor offered to pray. The mom agreed that it would be fine for them to pray. And she specifically mentioned that her young son had a heart defect he'd struggled with since birth. And so the pastor and the other Christians prayed over this family in the name of *Isa al Masih*, and then left the home and continued on with their aid delivery. At the end of the day they returned to their city.

A few days later, the pastor's phone rings. It's the mom who received the aid, the one whose son they'd prayed over.

"I need you to write down the prayer that you prayed for my son," she told the pastor.

He was a bit confused. "Okay, I guess I can write it down. But can you tell me why you need to have the prayer written down?"

"It's the heart murmur that my son had, the one he's had since birth. The heart murmur is gone now! The doctors say there's no sign that he's ever had any heart issues at all! I need you to write down the prayer you prayed, because I want to say that prayer over my other children as well."

Muslims are told exactly what to say to Allah, and when to say it. This woman had seen Jesus heal her son, so she would be praying to Him now, since she'd seen that He actually answers prayers. But she wanted to be sure she would say the right words to Him!

Aqil smiled with delight and praised the Lord for His healing touch on the boy. And he explained to this mother that it wasn't any special words that were said that led to her son's healing. It was *who* the words were said to. Jesus Christ, the Son of God, was the One to whom he had prayed on behalf of her son, and it was He who had heard their prayers, answered them, and brought healing to the little boy's heart.

It didn't take long for that mother to decide that she wanted to follow *Isa al Masih*, the One who hears and answers our prayers.

When Aqil told me the story, he was actually a bit sheepish. He had, after all, argued with God that he was far too busy to add refugee ministry to his weekly schedule. And besides, there were people from his own country who needed God. Couldn't God send someone else to work with the Syrians?

Yet over and over after he accepted the task, he'd seen God move in mighty ways. Muslim refugees were often confused that people of their own faith wouldn't help them. Yet these Christians would. Aqil saw God's hand at work. He'd seen God provide for needs, often miraculously. He'd seen the sick made well. And he'd seen Muslims—even Islamic leaders—leave Islam to follow Jesus. These stories were not once-a-year wonders; they were becoming weekly occurrences, almost expected.

The time he spent working with refugees had become Aqil's favorite time of the week. It was the place he felt most fulfilled in his work. It was the place God seemed to move most clearly and often. In the ministry service he'd tried to avoid, he now found utter excitement and joy.

FOR REFLECTION

When Aqil was first offered the chance—and funding—to work with Syrian refugees, he turned it down: "No, thank you." The opportunity didn't fit with his plans. Yet God gently prodded him to say yes, and that area of ministry has become Aqil's most fruitful and satisfying.

Certainly, Aqil is not alone in responding this way. Jonah literally ran (or sailed, rather) away from the calling God placed on his life. Moses prayed, "Oh, my Lord, please send someone else" (Ex. 4:13). We can't say yes to every opportunity someone brings our way. But when God is clearly leading, we must choose to follow His voice and call.

Has God opened a door for you that you've chosen not to walk through? Has He called you to do something, and you've said "No, thank you"? Take time to reflect on why. Write down what's holding you back from a willing "Yes." Consider whether He might be offering you a pathway to experience His hand working in mighty ways, a pathway to joy and fulfillment beyond your expectations.

PRAYER

Father, show me the path You have for me to walk, and help me hear Your voice, discern Your will, and always be willing to say yes to Your call. Allow me to see Your power in the areas in which I'm involved, and to be Your representative to those around me in every situation.

For Your Journal

_____

_____

_____

_____

_____

_____

_____

_____

_____

From a Post-Trip Prayer Letter

Here were some highlights of my trip:

- Hearing about the openness of refugees to the gospel message; Christians delivering aid tell the refugees they want to pray for them in Jesus' name. Very few refugees ever say no. And there have been healings and miracles and people coming to Christ.

- Seeing a refugee outreach that includes a medical clinic, a dental clinic, a school, and vocational training. Literally hundreds of lives are being impacted each week by this one ministry that VOM is blessed to partner with.

- Visiting the home of a Syrian refugee woman and her two kids. This was a heartbreaking visit, because this Muslim woman seems to have no hope. Her husband left her, her children are traumatized by what they've seen in Syria. But she was pleased to welcome people from the church that are reaching out to her. We prayed before we left that she would know God's love for her and that He would provide for her and her children.

THE PRISON BIBLE

Therefore, if anyone is in Christ, he is a new creation. The old has passed away; behold, the new has come.

2 CORINTHIANS 5:17

....

Turkey, 2016

"My dad is such an evangelist. If he witnessed to this salt shaker, this salt shaker would get saved!"

We sat around the table at a rooftop restaurant on the European side of Istanbul, an amazingly beautiful view in every direction. A turn of the head takes your eyes from the Hagia Sophia to the Blue Mosque to the Bosporus, with ships passing to and fro in the distance.

The family we were meeting—dad and mom, grown son and his wife, and teenaged daughter—had fled from Iran a few months earlier.

The dad, Houmayoun, had been a drug addict in Iran, hopelessly addicted like so many others in a country with one of the highest addiction rates in the world. Then Jesus came to him in a dream, and when Houmayoun woke up his addiction was gone. He no longer had any desire for drugs. This miracle convinced him that Jesus was much more than a prophet, but indeed the Son of God.

The Son of God who speaks to us, and heals us! Who wouldn't want to follow Him?

Without the daily use of drugs, his health improved dramatically. But the change in his spirit was even more significant.

You might think Houmayoun's wife—seeing her husband no longer taking drugs, and now treating her much better than he had previously—would be excited. But Houmayoun's wife was enraged. How could he bring such shame on her and their entire family by leaving Islam to follow Jesus?

Her family encouraged her to divorce him, but she wasn't quite ready to let go of her marriage and her husband. She left Houmayoun for a time, but the obvious change in his life and heart slowly won her back. Eventually, she also chose to follow Jesus, and their home became a gospel lighthouse in their city in Iran. Houmayoun could especially identify with, and had a heart to reach, drug addicts. He began reaching out and seeing other addicts accept Christ and give up their drugs.

He was a natural evangelist. Every conversation he had seemed to lead into a discussion of faith and how Jesus was the God who answers prayers. (I don't believe, though, he ever actually talked to a salt shaker!)

The waiter brought more tea to our table, and the conversation halted temporarily as he refilled our glasses and sugar cubes were distributed around the table. A white seagull stood sentry on the roof of the building next door.

You might think helping drug addicts get clean would be lauded by local authorities. Not in Iran, not if Jesus is involved. In the eyes of police and religious officials, Houmayoun wasn't helping drug addicts. He was encouraging apostasy, and that is a crime. He was sent to prison.

In prison Houmayoun was without a Bible, but he found other

believers inside the jail, and they quickly addressed the need for a Bible. A blank notebook was circulated to each of the imprisoned Christians, and each wrote down the verses he had memorized before his arrest. For the three years Houmayoun was in prison, that notebook was his (and the others') Bible.

Houmayoun wasn't the only one who suffered for his faith. After his arrest, his wife was arrested, for she, too, was involved in their house church leadership and in leading other women to Christ. Their son, Haidar, spent his eighteenth birthday in prison because he also was telling other Iranians about the Jesus who had completely healed his dad from drug addiction.

When he was released from prison, Houmayoun continued the ministry work God had laid before him. But it became more difficult. The authorities monitored him everywhere; continuing his work was putting other Christians at risk.

With heavy hearts, the family made the decision to leave Iran. They crossed into Turkey, where they had no status and had to work through the long immigration process before being allowed to legally work.

But Houmayoun's gospel work in Iran didn't stop just because he wasn't physically in the country. Every evening he was in front of his computer screen, talking via video chat with Christians in Iran, discipling and instructing church leaders and encouraging them to continue their vital ministry.

An evangelist doesn't stop evangelizing just because he is out of his home country. Houmayoun was rapidly adding to his Turkish vocabulary and beginning to have gospel conversations with Turks as well—at the grocery store, the restaurant, or wherever he encountered people in need of Christ. It was in telling these stories that Haidar, translating for his parents, made the laughing boast that his dad could even witness to the salt shaker!

"So what is your future?" we asked, expecting them to say that they were working through the United Nations refugee process and waiting for their chance to come to the West. Their answer surprised us: they were hoping to go back to Iran. Yes, they wanted to go back to the nation that had imprisoned and harassed them. But they didn't see a nation that had imprisoned them. Instead, they saw millions of Iranians imprisoned by Islam, waiting to know that there is a Savior ready and willing to free and heal them and bring them into fellowship with Him.

How could a man with an evangelist's heart leave when there was so much work still to be done?

FOR REFLECTION

How has Jesus changed you? What parts of your old, "before Christ," life are gone? How have you become a "new creation"? Not just since your salvation. How has Jesus changed you in the last twelve months or the last sixty days? What areas is He sculpting right now to shape or stretch you to be more like Him? For your journal, write down how God has changed you (a spouse or close friend may see areas that aren't as clear to you).

Have you told anyone recently about those changes? People might argue with your logic, with the authority of Scripture, or with some other means of convincing them intellectually to accept Christ. But it's very hard for them to argue with your experience, with your story. Houmayoun tells the story of how he was a drug addict for years, and then how he met Jesus and all the desire for drugs was gone in a moment. Who can argue with that? And who wouldn't want to meet that Jesus?

Ask God for an opportunity to tell someone this week how He has worked in your life.

PRAYER

Jesus, thank You for bold evangelists like Houmayoun. Please help me recognize the amazing changes You've wrought in my life, and help me tell someone this week about how You have changed, and are still changing, me to be more like You.

Watch over and protect my brothers and sisters in Iran, and bring many more Iranians to faith in You. Amen.

For Your Journal

_____

_____

_____

_____

_____

_____

_____

_____

_____

_____

From a Post-Trip Prayer Letter

My trip was wonderful! It included great opportunities to meet with brothers and sisters serving Christ on the front lines in hard places, as well as fun opportunities to see beautiful sites and historic places that are world-renowned.

One highlight was meeting a family from Iran; the father spent more than three years in prison, the mother spent almost a year in prison, and even the son was arrested for his Christian faith and as a way to punish his parents (he "celebrated" his eighteenth birthday in jail). Jesus saved the father from thirty-plus years of drug addiction, and in prison he ministered to other drug addicts and even to death-row inmates. He said in prison he came to understand how God can use suffering to bless a person.

"WE ALL KNOW"

> For it has been granted to you that for the sake of Christ you should not only believe in him but also suffer for his sake.
>
> **PHILIPPIANS 1:29**

....

China, 2010s

My host in China had arranged for me to meet with one of VOM's Bible delivery partners. I don't remember now if he never told me his name, or if I left it out of my notes so that I'd quickly forget, and so if my notes were somehow confiscated it wouldn't be there for anyone to find. For clarity's sake here, I'll call him Mr. Xi, though he was not, I can assure you, China's president.

One of the ways VOM serves persecuted Christians in many places is to provide them with God's Word. It is their second request, after our prayers. The writer of Hebrews said the Word of God is "living and active" (4:12), and our brothers and sisters who suffer for the name of Christ crave access to that life. In China, standing with our persecuted brothers and sisters means VOM is delivering Bibles to Christians in every province across the nation, using every means possible.

Mr. Xi came to us at night. It would have been too dangerous for him if we had gone to him. He was soft-spoken and calm; my quick impression was that this was not a man who would get rattled, ever. As he told his story, I came to understand why. Persecution, it seems, runs in his family.

His grandfather was a house church pastor and a missionary to other parts of China after the Communist takeover in 1949. Eventually, Grandpa Xi spent more than ten years in prison. Mr. Xi was quick to make sure we understood that his grandfather's time in prison was actually short; many church leaders of that era spent more than two decades in prison.

Mr. Xi's father was a deacon in the church. He also was detained by police on many occasions. My new friend told me that when he was a child, there were very few cars where they lived. So the few times they saw a car coming down their street, it usually meant authorities were coming to arrest his father. Mr. Xi said when they saw a car coming, his father would calmly ask his mother to collect some extra clothes for him to take with him, in case his "visit" to the police station turned into days or weeks in prison.

Growing up in such a home, it's no surprise that Mr. Xi is also involved in gospel work. And because of his front-row understanding of the costs of ministering for Christ in China, Mr. Xi wasn't surprised or deterred when he was asked to pay a price as well. In fact, he sees benefits in persecution.

"Persecution is like fire," he told me. "I use the word like *purify*. If we want pure gold, we have to let it go through fire." He said that Christianity had become "cool" among Chinese people who thought of it as a Western religion, and thought all parts of Western culture were popular or cool.

"The blessing [of persecution] for the church is that when we are facing the difficulties, the serious believers will stay. So it doesn't matter what happens." Persecution leaves the church full of believers serious about their faith—serious enough that threats of arrest or physical pain can't keep them from meeting. Those who are there only because it's "cool" quickly fall away.

Churches full of pure, refined gold tend to be unstoppable.

Mr. Xi is one of those believers. Following his family footsteps, he's been detained by police on many occasions, and several times served fifteen days of "administrative detention." I asked him about the first time he was arrested, and the first word he used was *privilege*.

"I am finally like my grandfather!" Mr. Xi said. "The interesting thing is five years of his prison [time] was in [deleted for security] Province, and what happened to me was in the same province and very close to where my grandfather was [imprisoned].

"I felt like I am so privileged in my family. Many years ago, my grandfather was here and suffered for the Lord, and today I am here. I just felt a privilege, and also my father was so happy. He said, 'Many years ago, I came here to pick up your grandfather, and today I am picking up you from the same province very close to each other.' He was like, 'Lord, thank you. I thank you.'"

It took me a moment to process what Mr. Xi had just said. How many American parents, including me, would be *thankful* that our children were arrested and spent time in prison? But Mr. Xi explained further:

> I think Christianity is really a relationship, and God is real, and we have this relationship with Him. And it is not just by saying, "Okay, God, we trust You." We trust Him and know the Great Commission He has given us, so we are so honored to be His servants. I don't see any reason we shouldn't be happy. This is really a great blessing from Him.
>
> By the way, you can save people. There are people in the prison, they are really hopeless people and they are facing a

death sentence and they will be leaving [this] world [soon]. You have the chance to share the gospel with them and save their souls from death. What a blessing the first time I really experienced the miracle happening in that beautiful time.

From Xi's very first visit to prison, he has kept that attitude. And today, he knows his Bible distribution work could send him back to prison for three years—or more. It's not an outcome he's losing sleep over.

"I mean, persecution and suffering, you can't really hide from it. If you are a real Christian, you will be persecuted. It doesn't matter—you will be persecuted if you want to be a godly person (see 2 Tim. 3:12).

"We all know if we choose to work for the Lord, sometime, maybe not now, you will be persecuted for sure."

We finished our conversation, said our goodbyes, and Mr. Xi departed. His retreating figure merged quickly into the darkness, going back to his family and his ministry work, and quite possibly, I know, to further arrests, imprisonment, and persecution. As I watched him go, I wished that thinking about future hardship left me as unfazed as it does this bold brother in the Lord.

FOR REFLECTION

Mr. Xi, like so many of our family members in hostile and restricted nations, has already counted the cost of following Christ. "We all know," he says, that persecution will come. So when it comes, it's not a surprise that throws these bold Christians off stride or crumbles their faith. They've prepared for its arrival, and when it comes, their perspective is already decided: that it is a privilege to suffer for the Christ who suffered for us.

How can you, in your context (and likely in your comfort), count the cost of following Christ ahead of time (see Luke 14:28)? What is it worth to you? What has it already cost you? What would you *willingly and joyfully* give up to keep walking with Jesus? For your journal, write down your list—and how you can think of each sacrifice as a privilege—as a way of counting the cost of following Christ.

PRAYER

Jesus, I want to want You more than I want anything else. Help me count the cost and make the decision, to set in my mind and my heart that *You are all I need* and more valuable to me than family, friendships, material things, comfort, or anything else that might distract me from You.

For Your Journal

From My Journal

The high-speed trains are really cool . . . and fast. And they have REAL POTTIES on them now! No more squatty that just falls down onto the tracks. It's more like an airplane potty with the airlock and sucking sound. But it has a seat and a bowl!

(Author's note: YES, I really do write in my journal about the quality of the bathrooms!)

Listen

You can hear my conversation with "Brother Xi" at www.VOMRadio.net/weknow.

QUOTES TO CONSIDER

Christianity doesn't deny the reality of suffering and evil. Remember after Jesus came down the Mount of Trans-figuration, He told His disciples that he was going up to Jerusalem—that He would be executed and that He would triumph over death. Jesus was not the least bit confident that He would be spared suffering. He knew that suffering was necessary. What He was confident of was vindica-tion. Our hope, our acceptance of the invitation to the banquet, is not based on the idea that we are going to be free of pain and suffering. Rather it is based on the convic-tion that we will triumph over suffering. . . .

Christian hope stands firm and serene, confident even in the face of the gas chamber, even in the face of terminal cancer. However serious we believe Good Friday is, we are confident that Easter Sunday lies ahead of us. And what if we do die? Jesus died too, and if Jesus died we believe that now He lives, and that we shall live too.

—Brennan Manning[4]

Count it all joy, my brothers, when you meet trials of various kinds, for you know that the testing of your faith produces steadfastness. And let steadfastness have its full effect, that you may be perfect and complete, lacking in nothing.

James 1:2–4

DAY 21

A DOUBLE PORTION —PART 1

As the Lord has forgiven you, so you also must forgive.
COLOSSIANS 3:13

....

Malatya, Turkey, May 2007

Certain stories of persecution become personal for me. This is true for others on staff at VOM as well, though usually what becomes personal for them is different from what becomes such for me. One of those stories that somehow became firmly attached to my heart was the martyrdom of three Christians in the office of a Christian publishing house in the city of Malatya, Turkey, in April 2007.

The initial media reports of the killings were sensationalized. Early reports said parts of their bodies had been cut off by the killers and suggested their suffering, prior to their deaths, was beyond imagination.

I read those reports online, not knowing God would allow me personal interaction with these men's families. After reading these gruesome reports in my office, sitting around our dinner table that evening, I was reading our family devotion, which came from the story of Elisha taking the mantle from Elijah. In reading that story, my mind went to Turkey and the unimaginable suffering of my brothers there. And, sitting at the table, the dinner dishes not yet cleared away, I began to weep. My wife and two sons stared at me, wondering, perhaps, if I was finally cracking up.

As we prayed after reading the Scripture passage, a thought came to my mind and I prayed that the five children left fatherless by this act of violence in Turkey would receive—just as Elisha had—a double portion of their fathers' spirit, the spirit that made these men willing to lay down their lives for Christ rather than deny Him or even live an easier life in a "safe" place to serve Him.

Seven weeks after that dinner, I stood outside the door of the Zirve publishing company in Malatya. There was a police car parked outside the building, and my hosts told me it would be unwise to stay long. I was sobered by the thought that, just on the other side of the dark wood door, three of my brothers had their throats slit simply for being followers of Christ. Two of them were Turkish; they were called the first martyrs of the modern Turkish church. The other man was a German Christian; he'd moved to Turkey to serve the people and to shine as a gospel lighthouse in that culture.

The men who killed them had posed as "seekers," interested in knowing more about the Christian faith and maybe even becoming followers of Christ. Some of them had even come to services at the church. All five were arrested at the scene of the murders; in their pockets they carried notes that they were defending their country and their religion—Islam.

My trip to Turkey had come about quickly. A friend of a friend there would take me to Malatya. I could meet with Susanne Geske, the widow of the German man, Tilmann. When I got there, I found there were challenges. It seemed as if Susanne might not see me after all.

But I called, and then we went to her apartment, and she welcomed me inside. We talked about her husband, his murder, and her response. She, along with the other widow (the third murdered man was engaged but not yet married), had offered forgiveness to her husband's killers on national TV in Turkey only *hours* after the murders. How could she do that? I asked her that very question: "A lot has been said about the fact that you have forgiven these men, and even on national television you have forgiven them. How were you able to do that?"

Susanne told me, "The thing is, on the first day lots of people were here from all over Turkey. The Turkish Protestant Christians, lots of people. So they said the television station is coming. They said, 'Do you want to say anything?' And I was like, 'What should I say?' I was like, 'Huh?' They said, 'You can say something good. What is in your heart?'"

"So this was the day after—twenty-four hours later, basically?" I asked.

"Not even," she replied. "I had not had a single second of anger or anything in my heart—nothing. Just nothing. I was like, 'This is not normal.' My little daughter, she was jumping around and shouting about all these bad Turks, about how she wanted to go back to Germany, and about how it's all so bad. And I thought, *This is funny, she's really angry*. And I wasn't even angry—nothing. I thought it was interesting. Actually, they really didn't know what they did, [that thought] came to my mind. And then I thought, *There's a verse in the Bible*. And so I said, 'I actually can forgive them. Because the Lord forgave me so much, so I have to forgive them.'

"And there is really nothing against them. I can't say I have anything against them. Maybe it will come, a time of grieving, and I will have a time of anger and all this stuff. But I think it's still . . . I can forgive them because they really didn't know what they do. If you hear about what the police say and what they all say, they really didn't know. They have no clue what that meant, what they were . . . And I just could say, 'I forgive them, happily.' Because the Lord forgave me and . . ."

"So really you just felt like it was an honor . . ." I said.

"It was from the Lord," Susanne said. "Sorry, you can't do this on your own. No way."

FOR REFLECTION

You can't do this on your own. Susanne's experience is, in my observation, not the usual. Most Christians I've interviewed who have faced intense persecution weren't able to forgive so quickly. In most cases, there is a wrestling process they went through, trying to forgive and trying to give the bitterness or anger they feel over to God and allowing Him to take it permanently from them. It's likely that many readers of this book will have been through something traumatic. Someone wronged or abused you or in some other way put you in a place of needing to forgive.

And it's hard! It's hard to relieve someone of responsibility for their actions—"they know not what they do" (Luke 23:34)—for the pain and harm they caused. In fact, it's impossible. *You can't do this on your own.* Whether it happens instantaneously, like it did for Susanne, or over weeks, months, or even years, it is God who does the work. It is His grace that enables us to forgive.

For your journal, write about areas in your life where you need Him to do this work. How long has that need existed?

PRAYER

Dear Lord Jesus, thank You for forgiving my sin; not lightly or easily but with Your own pain and suffering on the cross, taking my guilt on Your divine, sinless head and paying the price for all my sin.

God, as You have forgiven me, right now I choose to forgive
_____, who wronged me by _____
_____
_____.

Lord, I choose to forgive this person, but I need Your help! Take from me the anger, bitterness, and resentment I feel. Enable me, with Your supernatural power, to love this person who wronged me, to demonstrate to them the same, full forgiveness that You gave me. Help me now, and tomorrow, and the next day, and all the days after that not to pick this anger and bitterness back up but to truly forgive, as You modeled for me.

For Your Journal

_____
_____
_____
_____
_____
_____
_____

From My Journal

It seems each international departure is a bit more difficult than the last one. Char said today that's 'cause I think my luck is running out . . . but I don't think it's that. I think that each year that goes by, I realize that my life is passing, that my time with Kameron and Kedrick at home is growing much shorter.

The travel is hard, because there's way too much time just to sit and think and be homesick. Once I get there and hit the ground and get busy, it won't be such an issue, because my mind will be busier.

DAY 22

A DOUBLE PORTION —PART 2

Father of the fatherless and protector of widows is God in his holy habitation.

PSALM 68:5

. . . .

Malatya, Turkey, 2007

She was beautiful, but she seemed delicate and fragile.

She was utterly heartbroken.

Being single and a Christian in Turkey is a tricky path to walk. The church is so small in this country of seventy-plus million people that one's chance, as a single Christian, of finding the ideal single Christian of the opposite sex and falling in love is small. Add to that the challenge of Muslim families, often openly hostile to converts, and it's a challenging road.

But this young woman had walked that path, and found true love. It was only months until they would be husband and wife.

But before that glorious, God-honoring day could come, her fiancé was murdered—one of three men killed in the offices of a

Christian publishing company in Malatya, Turkey. Now I sat across the table from her. That afternoon, I'd visited his grave and talked with his Muslim parents, who were still bewildered and angry that their son had left Islam and that he'd been so brutally murdered.

Her emotions were all over the place during our team's dinner with her. She showed us a video of her fiancé, Uğur Yüksel, on her phone. He was clowning and dancing in his chair. I don't speak Turkish, but he clearly was having a good time when that video was taken. She smiled and laughed as she watched it, her eyes glowing with love and the tears of loss just below the surface.

"He was so kind," she told us, a noticeable thing in their culture. He treated her well. He was warm and funny. And he loved God—even when his family ostracized him. Even when long-time friends turned away from him. He loved Jesus; he wanted to serve Him the rest of his life, and he'd asked her to join him in that service.

Then he was gone. Uğur was still alive when police burst through the door of the publishing house. He was taken by ambulance to the hospital. But his wounds were too great, he'd lost too much blood. His life here on earth couldn't be saved. His life in eternity with Christ began. But he left behind this devastated young woman, her broken heart leaking from the corners of her eyes and sliding down her cheeks.

Later, my host would explain that her suffering, in the seven weeks since the murders, had been great. Before the killings—front-page news all over Turkey—it wasn't widely known that she was a Christian. Even some members of her own family didn't know. Now not only was it known, but her name and address were published in local media, making her a target to those who would want to "influence" her to return to Islam, or commend the killing of her "infidel" fiancé.

But that wasn't her only burden. In Turkish culture, it was explained to me, for her to openly show her heartbreak would impugn her character; why would you weep and cry over this young man, unless your relationship had been physically consummated?

So she had to be careful how much of her grief she would allow to show outside the small circle of the Christian community there. Even with her own family, most of her heartbreak must stay hidden.

And once the heartbreak began to heal, once the tears dried up, what was the chance of her finding another Christian young man?

It is natural and common for us—whether "us" is Western Christians, the (comparatively) wealthy, VOM workers, or, I think, men—to want to step in and help when we see a situation of such suffering. The creative part of my brain was quickly shuffling through ideas of how to "rescue" this damsel in distress. Could we move her to a bigger city, where more Christians were? What if she married an American and moved to America, out of danger and beyond the reach of her persecutors?

But she wasn't looking for "rescue," and, realistically, it wasn't something I or my coworkers could offer. What we could offer is fellowship. We could offer to buy her dinner and sit and laugh as we watched videos on her phone of Uğur. We could offer her a tissue when the tears flowed. We could listen as she shared about the stress of everyone in the whole country suddenly knowing that she had left Islam and was an "infidel" follower of Jesus of Nazareth. And we could pray with her, and for her, as she navigated the choppy, lonely waters she found herself in.

I've not seen that young woman since she left the restaurant that evening, now more than thirteen years ago, in central Turkey. I heard she later got married, but I don't know much more than that. I hope the heartbreak I saw that night has been swept away by great joy in the intervening years. I hope she looks to God as her protector (see Ps. 68:5), that she knows He is looking out for her best and that she experiences His provision for her needs, contentment, and well-being.

FOR REFLECTION

It's easy to want to "rescue" someone we see in distress or suffering. But sometimes we must instead make peace that we cannot rescue and instead actively choose to fellowship. Is there someone you've been trying to rescue whom you should instead choose to listen to, laugh with, cry with, and pray with? For your journal, prayerfully consider if you are trying to rescue when you should be trying to fellowship instead. Write out your prayer for that person, entrusting them to the Lord. Then make a point to reach out to them in fellowship.

PRAYER

Lord, allow me to carry the soothing balm of Your love into every relationship I have or develop. Grant me discernment to know when I should try to rescue, and when I should seek fellowship instead. Allow me to serve by listening, laughing or crying together, and by praying with those in need of your grace and wisdom. Amen.

For Your Journal

_____

_____

_____

_____

_____

_____

_____

_____

_____

From My Journal

After that, we actually went to the building. There was a police car out front, but we walked in and took stills and video of the office door—it's still closed off. It was a bit weird—the journalist in me wanting to document the story, the Indiana Jones loving the adrenaline rush of walking in right in front of the police van, but the Christian in me in awe to think that on the other side of this door, three of my brothers were tortured to death while gracefully encouraging five guys with knives to stop being evil, repent of their sins, and follow Christ.

DAY 23

A DOUBLE PORTION —PART 3

Instead of your shame there shall be a double portion; instead of dishonor they shall rejoice in their lot; therefore in their land they shall possess a double portion; they shall have everlasting joy.

ISAIAH 61:7

....

Istanbul, Turkey, 2007

After my visit to Malatya and central Turkey, I flew back to Turkey's largest city. Semse Aydin, the second woman left a widow by the attack at the Christian publishing house, was living with relatives near Istanbul. The plan was for a pastor friend to pick me up at the airport and we'd go interview her.

He picked me up on schedule, and we began to drive. His cell phone rang, and he answered it. Within 20 seconds, in spite of understanding no more than five Turkish words, I could tell it wasn't good news.

The pastor didn't speak a lot of English, but he didn't need much to communicate the message of the phone call. "She say no come. She too tired."

My heart fell. *I had flown six thousand miles to visit*, I selfishly thought. *Couldn't she see me today and rest up tomorrow?*

But—in a way that, honestly, isn't normal for me—I quickly transitioned to thankfulness. My trip was already a rousing success. I'd interviewed Susanne. I'd met Uğur's fiancée and parents. I'd gotten great material to share with VOM's magazine readers, with radio audiences, and anyone else who would listen. My heart had been touched and inspired. Even without this last interview, my trip was a big success in terms of my VOM responsibilities.

"Thank you, Lord," I silently prayed. "Thank You for the meetings You've allowed me to have; bless Semse with rest today and comfort her in her loss, and allow me to travel safely home and share well the stories of these amazing believers."

With my schedule suddenly wide open, the pastor and I headed to a local restaurant for a late breakfast. We were enjoying as much conversation as we could with my limited Turkish and his limited English when his phone rang again.

He talked in Turkish. He looked at me and smiled and nodded his head. He hung up.

"She says come for little. Maybe one hour."

I'd done interviews in less than an hour before. "Hallelujah!" I said. That word is apparently the same in Turkish, because my pastor friend repeated it: "Hallelujah!"

We finished breakfast quickly and got in the car; about ninety minutes later we met an American sent to screen me (I learned that part later), and also to serve as my translator. I must've passed this final test, because soon I was in an apartment meeting Semse, her two children, and her relative they were staying with. Semse's English at that time was limited, but her relative was fluent.

"This is Esther," Semse introduced me to her young daughter, who was shy and unsure who this foreigner was and whether he could be trusted. "And this is Elisha."

For a few seconds, it was as if I couldn't catch my breath. *Elisha!*
The story of these three men who had given their lives for Christ
in Malatya had lodged itself in my heart around my own dinner table as my family and I read the story of Elisha. I'd prayed since that
evening that five children would receive a double portion of their
fathers' martyr spirit, just as Elisha had received a double portion of
Elijah's. And now I was meeting the last of those children, and his
name was Elisha!

My hosts clearly wondered why there were suddenly tears in the
corners of my eyes, so I had to tell the story. I think God used that
story to make a connection between us, because my visit wasn't for
one hour; it was more like eight. Semse shared her story and her
heart, and even pulled out her Bible to share some of the Scriptures
God had used to get her through the previous seven weeks. There
was laughter, tears, food, and fellowship. It wasn't long before I felt
I'd become part of this family.

Semse painted for me a picture of her husband, Necati, the pastor
of the young church in Malatya, and the man who'd opened the
door of the office that fateful morning for his five killers, expecting
"seekers" interested in learning more about Christ.

Giving his life wasn't Necati's first sacrifice for Christ. In fact, his
Muslim family turned against him after the woman he was interested
in dating—Semse—led him to become a follower of Jesus. During
his military service, his fellow soldiers and officers were determined
to make him so miserable he'd drop Christianity and return to his
roots, to Islam. They failed to crack his resolve. After leaving the
military, he'd been arrested while distributing Christian books.

Some of those who would be his killers had visited their church.
They'd feigned interest in the gospel, asked lots of questions, and
called to set up private meetings. Necati wasn't convinced their in-

terest was real; he didn't completely trust them. But he went to the office that morning to meet with them, to answer their questions and invite them to see "the Way, the Truth and the Life."

He was tired that last morning; he'd just returned from a trip. "So why go?" Semse had asked him. "Why waste your time?"

"Because," he told her, "even if their motives aren't true, at least they will hear the gospel."

They might just be trying to cause trouble, or get the church closed down, but even if that were so, their attempt was an opening. And Necati would take advantage of every opening to preach Christ.

The Easter before his death, Necati had been part of the cast for a play, put on by the believers in Malatya, depicting the Easter story. He'd portrayed Christ, including being "nailed" to the cross and lifted up by the soldiers. No one there knew that Necati would soon represent Christ again, this time shedding his own blood and giving his life.

As we sat in the living room of that apartment, Semse, too, talked about forgiving the five men who'd taken her husband from her. She echoed Susanne's story that it was God's power that had enabled her to do so. Certainly, it wasn't her own. And she shared that her willingness to sacrifice grew directly out of her deep love for Jesus, the One who had saved her and transformed the Muslim man she'd met on a bus into her godly husband and the father of her children. It is an honor, she told me, to die for Christ. And it was an honor, she said, to have been married to a man that God would choose and bless with the gift of martyrdom.

When we left that apartment for the drive back to my hotel, my heart was overwhelmed with thanksgiving. God had opened the door for me to meet and interview all three women most affected by the attack in Malatya. He'd allowed me to both laugh and cry with them, to fellowship in Christ's suffering (Phil. 3:10) with these Turkish members of Christ's body.

And I had the strong sense that God had called *me*, personally. Not just anyone, and not even a representative of VOM. From the day I'd wept at the dinner table to hearing the words, "This is Elisha," God's fingerprints were all over this trip. I was the one traveling, but my itinerary was obviously one He had designed.

I smiled at my pastor friend as he drove and said again the Turkish word I'd learned that day: "Hallelujah!"

"Hallelujah!" he replied with a laugh. "Hallelujah!"

My heart was full, and I was ready to go home. But God had one more opportunity in store for me in Turkey before I boarded my flight.

FOR REFLECTION

Is there some area God has called you to that you've given up on as a "waste of time"? The person at work who's just completely closed to Christ's love? The unglamorous ministry that seemingly *never* really makes a difference? The person you've talked to twenty-five times before, without even a hint of fruit, so you *know* it'd be a waste of time to talk to them a twenty-sixth time? Necati Aydin was willing to "waste his time" if it meant someone would hear the gospel. He suspected the young men who came as "seekers" to his church weren't being completely honest. Yet he went to meet them, reasoning that even if they were just looking for trouble, they would still hear the gospel, and it's *never* a waste of time when someone hears the gospel.

For your journal, write down the names of your "waste of time" people. From this day forward, each time you think of or interact with those persons, remember the faithful example of Necati Aydin, and persevere!

PRAYER

Father, let me always remember that my moments and my days
are in Your hands. You are establishing the pathway before me.
Let me never see the tasks You give or the people You bring my
way as a "waste of time," but let me always see them as opportunities to represent You and opportunities for someone—even
someone who seems uninterested—to hear the message of Your
love and Your Son's sacrifice for them.

For Your Journal

From My Journal

Semse said Necati had been arrested around 2000,
and held for a month in prison—while she was four months
pregnant. Semse said that after Necati got out of jail,
they sat down together and really talked about the
risks of serving the Lord 100 percent and being involved
in evangelism in Turkey. She said they talked about the
fact that they could work a normal job and go to church

and still be Christians—and probably avoid the risks of more jail time or trouble.

They decided—together—that they would follow Christ 100 percent and go and do anything that He called them to do, regardless of the risks.

From that day forward, the question was answered and they served the Lord completely.

PRAYING FOR PERSECUTED CHRISTIANS

At VOM, we often share stories about "frontline workers"—those sharing the gospel in hostile and restricted nations. I often use a different name for these brave men and women: pre-persecuted Christians. They're doing gospel work in places where those doing gospel work are targeted. They know the risks, and they keep going, answering God's call. For most, it's only a matter of time until they face persecution directly.

PRAY TODAY for frontline workers in hostile and restricted nations around the world. Pray for God's protection over them and their families. Pray for discernment as they make decisions about ministry and even make decisions about how to avoid drawing unwanted attention to their work. Pray for boldness to share the gospel, and fruit for their work.

A DOUBLE PORTION —PART 4

> I planted, Apollos watered, but God gave the growth. So neither he who plants nor he who waters is anything, but only God who gives the growth. He who plants and he who waters are one, and each will receive his wages according to his labor.
>
> **1 CORINTHIANS 3:6–8**

....

Istanbul, Turkey, 2007

After spending most of a day with Semse and her family, my heart was completely full. I felt overwhelmed by God's graciousness—to allow me to make this trip, to meet both widows and Uğur's fiancée and parents, to stand at the graves of two of the three martyrs, to share food and fellowship, to laugh and cry with these precious saints.

I had one day left before my early-morning flight home. I was in one of my favorite cities in the world, staying just down the hill from The Blue Mosque and the Hagia Sophia, two of the world's most beautiful and captivating structures. I figured I'd spend a relaxed final day being a tourist and getting ready to go home. But God had one more blessing for me before I left Turkey.

I had friends living in Istanbul at that time, and I'd sent them an email letting them know I'd be visiting their beautiful city. Their house was already full: a group of college students from the US was visiting, getting on-the-ground gospel experience in a Muslim country.

It was my privilege to join them for an afternoon and evening. It is (almost) always nice, as an American, to encounter other Americans in a foreign country. We enjoyed the fellowship of shared experience, language, and nationality. And awesome Turkish food!

At the end of the evening, I was asked to share for a few minutes about my trip, my work, and especially my time with the Malatya widows. I actually folded open the tiny screen of my video camera and showed the students some of the footage I'd shot of Susanne Geske sharing about her loss, how her faith made that loss bearable, and how only Christ's power enabled her to forgive her husband's killers.

My heart was full of admiration and sorrow at what my sisters in Turkey had suffered, and full of thankfulness that God had allowed me to be there, to meet them, and to help tell their story. As sometimes happens, my heart was so full, some of it began leaking from my eyes. I couldn't talk about the broken heart of Uğur's fiancée without part of my heart breaking on her behalf.

These students—people I'd never met before and haven't seen since—were so gracious to me. Their hearts were clearly also linked to the story of three men willing to die for Christ, and to the task of telling Turkish Muslims about Jesus.

One of my callings, I believe, is to amplify God's call to missions, to make clear that Christ's call to "go into all the world" (Mark 16:15) wasn't just for the disciples listening when He said it, but a call for all of His followers, through all time, to go places where Jesus' name has not been heard. One of my greatest blessings is when I hear that God used something I worked on—a book, a radio episode, a VOM newsletter article—to further someone's understanding that He was calling *them* to go.

When I left the students' hotel that night and walked back to my own—ten minutes away—I felt my time with them was one last blessing from God on this trip: the chance to plant missions seeds in the hearts of these students. That's a chance I try never to pass up!

I don't know what fruit, if any, came from those seeds. I've never seen any of those students again, and I don't know what they are doing or where they are. I was given an opportunity to speak into their lives, to plant seeds, and I did the best I could with God's help to make the most of that opportunity.

The next morning, I was on a plane headed home, still glowing inside with the sense that God had brought me—personally—to Turkey to meet with these believers, to hear their stories, and even to begin to share them. In the days after the trip I would have more opportunities to share about Susanne, Semse, and others I'd met in Turkey. There would be radio interviews in which I got to share about their faithfulness. I was asked to write an update for VOM's magazine. And, much later, I would be able to interview Semse for broadcast, helping her to share her story in her own words.

FOR REFLECTION

God doesn't put us in places or give us experiences without reason. And the reasons aren't just about our own faith walk, or shaping our own personal character. Often, the reason is for us to share that experience with others. God gives each of us experiences that produce faith seeds we can plant into the lives of people around us. Often, He will not only give us seeds, but bring specific people across our paths, at specific times, where we can sow those seeds of faith into already prepared soil.

We don't always know the results. We may not be part of watering that seed, be around when harvest comes, or even hear rumors that a harvest has happened. Our job is planting the seeds God gives us to plant.

I planted, Apollos watered, but God gave the increase.

For your journal: write about an experience in your life God has used to allow you to share His grace with others. Who can you share that story with this week?

PRAYER

Father, help me see how the experiences in my life provide seeds of faith to sow into the lives of others around me, and help me to be faithful to sow in every opportunity You give. Please bring eternal, spiritual fruit from the seeds I plant.

For Your Journal

_____

_____

_____

_____

_____

_____

_____

From My Journal

I think it was an opportunity to help water the seeds of missions and serving among persecuted Christians in [those students'] lives—now we'll see what fruit God produces. I feel like a part of my calling is to inspire people to think about missions, and so if I get that chance, I'll do it.

DAY 25

A DOUBLE PORTION —PART 5

> Declaring the end from the beginning and from ancient times things not yet done, saying, "My counsel shall stand, and I will accomplish all my purpose."
>
> **ISAIAH 46:10**

....

Colorado, Christmas Day, 2017

It's often only in hindsight we see most clearly the intricate ways God's hand is at work, His mighty plans unwinding through the years of our lives.

It was Christmas Day. Char and I gathered at her parents' home to celebrate the birth of Christ with family and friends. Across the piled-high Christmas dinner table from us sat Semse Aydin, along with her children, Esther and Elisha. The same family I'd met ten years before, when the scars of their loss and grief were so raw.

When I came home from Turkey just weeks after the Malatya killings in 2007, I had the distinct feeling that God had selected *me*, personally, to be the emissary from VOM to go and meet the widows and fiancée of the three martyred Christians, to hear their stories and come home to share those stories with the American church.

Now, sitting around the Christmas dinner table, I saw clearly one reason God might have had me go on that trip. God is outside of time; He sees ten years from today just as clearly as He sees today or ten years ago.

In the years after the deaths of my three brothers in Turkey, I had kept tabs, from a distance, on the two widows. Whenever I was in Turkey and spoke with people who knew them, I would ask how they were doing, where they were, what their lives were like. So I knew that not long after Necati was killed, his family had begun making noises that they wanted to take custody of his children, their grandchildren. They wanted to raise them to be good Muslims, unlike their infidel father.

It wasn't far-fetched to think a Muslim judge in a Turkish court might side with these grieving grandparents, and Semse—like any good mother—couldn't bear the thought of her children being taken away. She fled the country, eventually coming to the US. And out of all the places she could have ended up in her vast new homeland, she settled in Denver, Colorado.

My wife grew up in Colorado Springs, and her parents still live there. And so, one summer as we were making vacation plans, I made contact with Semse and asked if we could take her to lunch when we were in Colorado. She agreed.

We had other activities planned in Denver—I don't remember if it was the Museum of Nature & Science or Denver Broncos training camp—but we agreed to meet Semse and Esther and Elisha for lunch. This was probably 2011 or so. Char's folks—two of the most giving, godly people I've ever known—were with us for the day in Denver, and so they joined us for lunch.

Semse wanted us to meet at a Denny's. She later told us it was close enough to their apartment for them to walk. She still didn't feel comfortable driving in big-city traffic. We had lunch together. Her kids didn't say much: they weren't sure who these Americans were or why they wanted to have lunch. Semse remembered me coming to visit them in Turkey, but there had been many visitors in the weeks after Necati's death.

At the end of lunch, my in-laws told Semse, essentially, "Hey, we're just down the road in Colorado Springs. If you need help with anything, please call us." They traded phone numbers and email addresses, and off we went back to our vacation. I was glad to have seen Semse again; I hoped we'd been an encouragement to her. Little did I know my presence that day was nothing more than a bridge to connect her with my in-laws.

The next time my in-laws were in Denver, they called Semse. They went to lunch again. And then there was another lunch. Semse's car needed some work done, and my father-in-law has never found a car he cannot fix—although he'll deny this. In the months and years to come, there would be many meals, many conversations, laughter, and tears. Eventually, Semse decided to move—she now lives even closer to my in-laws.

In Denny's in Denver that day, a friendship was born. And it's a friendship that carries on to this day. My sons' grandparents have become a kind of adopted grandparents to Necati's children.

And so we found ourselves on Christmas Day gathered around the table, and I thought quietly back to that day in Turkey ten years before. A day when the first message was, "Semse's just too tired. Today isn't a good day to come." And then it was, "Go ahead and come for one hour." And now here we were, ten years and half-a-world away from that day in Turkey, our families together for Christmas dinner.

I don't remember if it was a prayer for the meal, or some other time that day, but my father-in-law asked Elisha to pray. He has a man's voice now, and he looks so much like the pictures I've seen of his father as a young man. Elisha began to pray—and it became very clear that this was a young man who knew the One to whom he was praying. This was a man on whom God's Spirit rested. This was a man carrying forward the legacy of a father who loved Jesus so much he was willing to lay down his life for Him.

And as he prayed, I wondered, *Is it possible my prayers from all those years ago have been answered? Is it possible that Elisha, this young man whose father was martyred for Christ, really did receive a double portion of his father's spirit?*

FOR REFLECTION

As you look back on your own life and walk of faith, are there places you see—in hindsight—God was clearly at work? Are there things that perhaps at the time you wondered about, or even complained about, but now you see were a divine foreshadowing of His work yet to come? Can you look back on prayers you prayed then and recognize how you now live in the fruit of God's answers? Take time today to write down those answered prayers, thank God for His handiwork, and celebrate the blessings that have grown out of walking the path He ordained for you.

Take time, also, to acknowledge that God may have much bigger plans connected to your circumstances today than what you see or know. Choose to accept and anticipate the intricate work of His hands, even though it may be years before you see the full extent of His design. Write out your feelings—even frustrations—about those situations. In the years to come, you can look back and see how God worked.

PRAYER

Father, thank You that You see the end from the beginning, that You are working Your will in my life and my circumstances. I choose to submit my will and my life to be used by You, in whatever way You see fit. Allow me, please, to see and celebrate the work You are doing and will do through me in the months and years to come.

For Your Journal

_____

_____

_____

_____

_____

_____

_____

_____

_____

_____

_____

_____

Listen

You can hear an interview with Semse Aydin, recorded at a VOM Advance Conference, at www.VOMRadio.net/Semse.

QUOTES TO CONSIDER

At the very heart of [early Christians'] view of reality was a man who died for his enemies, praying for their forgiveness. Reflection on this could only lead to a radically different way of dealing with those who were different from them.

—Timothy Keller[5]

Indeed, I count everything as loss because of the surpassing worth of knowing Christ Jesus my Lord. For his sake I have suffered the loss of all things and count them as rubbish, in order that I may gain Christ and be found in him, not having a righteousness of my own that comes from the law, but that which comes through faith in Christ, the righteousness from God that depends on faith—that I may know him and the power of his resurrection, and may share his sufferings, becoming like him in his death, that by any means possible I may attain the resurrection from the dead.

Philippians 3:8–11

DAY 26

"IF THE WHOLE WORLD BELIEVED"

"For God so loved the world, that he gave his only Son, that whoever believes in him should not perish but have eternal life. For God did not send his Son into the world to condemn the world, but in order that the world might be saved through him. Whoever believes in him is not condemned, but whoever does not believe is condemned already, because he has not believed in the name of the only Son of God."

JOHN 3:16–18

. . . .

Northwest China, 2003

It was the middle of winter and cold. And that was just *inside* our hotel! I slept with extra clothes on to try to stay warm. Outside, snow was falling.

We were near the far-western edge of China, and also in the midst of a battle. As is often the case under the Communist Party leadership in China, the battle was not for physical territory, but psychological territory. The Chinese government wants to control its people; government leaders want the first loyalty of every person to be the Party and the State.

In this part of China, the people are traditionally Muslim. Their first language is not the Mandarin Chinese of the Party, but the Turkic tongue *Uygur* ("we-gur"). To ensure control of the area, the Chinese government was importing thousands of ethnic Han Chinese people to drown out, or at least dilute, the Uygur cultural influence.

Being Uygur, in the eyes of the Chinese government, was one strike against you. Being a Christian and a Uygur? That meant trouble on every side.

We were tourists during the day, walking the streets, shopping in the bazaars and taking pictures everywhere. It was only after dark we could meet with Christians in this city; and we couldn't go to them; that would draw way too much attention. They came to us.

A man I'll call Ali was a student when he began to wonder about the tension between his Uygur people and the Han Chinese. He wondered if there was a way he could help his people avoid the heavy-handed oppression of the Chinese people and government. His first thought was that surely Islam would offer a way to do so.

As he was pondering these big questions, Ali met a Christian man. Ali told us he didn't particularly like the Christian, yet he found himself drawn almost inexplicably to the man's message. He began to study Christianity, wondering if maybe *this* was the thing which could bring peace to his people.

"I had discovered many bad things in Islam," Ali told us, "many things I couldn't accept. In Islam there was no justice or righteousness. So I began to study the Bible."

Ali's father was a leader of the local mosque. His brother had gone away to study Islam under the Taliban in Afghanistan. This was not a family that would easily accept one of its members showing interest in Christianity—and they didn't. When they discovered Ali was reading the Bible, they burned the book.

"Don't ever read that book again," they told him. "It's all wrong. It's all been changed."

The next day was the weekly day of prayer. As Ali's family prepared to go to the mosque, Ali announced that he would not be going with them. From that moment on, his family opposed him in every way. Soon after, he was kicked out of the family home.

"I am no longer your father," his father told him, "and you should *never* come home again."

But the family wasn't satisfied just to make Ali homeless. His father also visited his school, loudly complaining that staff clearly weren't monitoring the students, because if they were doing their jobs, his son wouldn't have become a Christian.

Fearing arrest, Ali dropped out of school and left the area. He moved to a place where he had relatives, but the relatives had been told by Ali's father he was no longer a Muslim, and they turned him away. Former friends also refused to welcome him or help him in any way.

Sleeping on the streets, or wherever he could, Ali soon became sick. He ended up in the hospital. Normally in China family members bring food to the patient, but Ali's family had deserted him. Yet even there, God provided. A sympathetic nurse brought food for him. Ali told us that without that food he would probably have died.

Sitting and hearing Ali's story, I could picture blow after blow to Ali's young faith. Yet he withstood every onslaught. He refused to back down. He refused to let go of Jesus. And at every point in his story, God sustained him.

When the bill for Ali's hospital stay came due, God provided funds to cover the amount. Now, out of school and with no home, Ali needed a job. But who would hire a young man who not only hadn't finished school, but also was a Christian? Miraculously, at just the right time, a job was offered to him. Every step of the way, Ali could see God's hands protecting and providing for him.

As a young student, Ali had wondered what could bring peace to his Uygur people. Now, he walked daily with the Prince of Peace, and longed to share Jesus with more of his people.

One of the questions I often ask persecuted Christians I meet is, *What is your favorite Bible verse?*

Ali's verse is one that probably every Christian can recite by heart: John 3:16.

"God says he loves *all* the people," Ali explained. "And I love that verse, because I love my people, too.

"If the whole world believed Christianity, there would be peace," he said.

FOR REFLECTION

Jesus warned us that His truth would divide families, and make us enemies, even in our own households:

> "For I have come to set a man against his father, and a daughter against her mother, and a daughter-in-law against her mother-in-law. And a person's enemies will be those of his own household. Whoever loves father or mother more than me is not worthy of me, and whoever loves son or daughter more than me is not worthy of me. And whoever does not take his cross and follow me is not worthy of me." (Matt. 10:35–38)

Perhaps you've never had to experience the truth of Jesus' words in this passage. Perhaps members of your family encouraged and inspired your walk of faith, and even today challenge you to be more like Christ. If that's your story, take time today to write a prayer of thanksgiving for that blessing. And take time to pray for those, like Ali, for whom following Christ means giving up their earthly family.

And if you're one of those who's been forced to choose between family and Jesus, know that you're not alone, and not forgotten. Jesus is willing and able to walk with and care for you just as He did Ali and so many others in restricted nations who have made that choice.

PRAYER

Jesus, help me value You above everything else, even my own family.

For Your Journal

From My Journal

The interesting thing is that the cold and snow weren't slowing business down. The stores—even the outside booths—were packed! Seems they must be used to snow and sub-zero temperatures here.

All of China is on one time zone. So way out here in the west the sun doesn't come up until almost 9 a.m. Seems crazy to me—but I'm sure that, from the Communist Party perspective, it makes it easier to control, manage, and dominate more than a billion people.

DAY 27

A FUNERAL SERMON

But in your hearts honor Christ the Lord as holy, always being prepared to make a defense to anyone who asks you for a reason for the hope that is in you; yet do it with gentleness and respect.

1 PETER 3:15

....

Central Asia, 2002

It was the first time I'd seen a man cry at the recall of his torture. The tears pooled in the corners of Pastor Ragimov's eyes, then slid out and down his cheeks. It was a hot summer day, but there was a breeze off the Caspian Sea as we sat outside his home, making it almost pleasant.

"I was beaten," he told us, his voice quiet but thick with emotion. "So many times, I was beaten."

But in the next breath, he told us that he prays for his persecutors. "I can't do anything about them," he said. "I just pray."

Much had changed in his country in the ten years since the Soviet Union came apart and his country gained independence. But one

thing hadn't changed: being a Christian and telling others about
Jesus would result in persecution. The people of central Asia were
coming out of seventy years of Communist domination, which included atheistic indoctrination and a distrust and mockery of any
and all religious expression.

But as Communism faded, what was rising in its place was an
Islamic identity that didn't like Christianity any more than the Communists had. The Communists thought Christians were troublemak-
ers; radical Muslims saw them as apostates worthy of death.

Pastor Ragimov was one of the first among his countrymen to follow Jesus. He'd seen the boot heel of Communist oppression, and he'd
seen the rising tide of radical Islam as well. He'd suffered under both.

Yet persecution and oppression couldn't stop him from sharing
about Jesus. If he was in a village, whatever the reason might be, he
assumed God wanted him to share the gospel with the villagers. If
police detained him, he assumed it was the policemen whom God
was trying to reach. And if a group of radical Muslims would accost
him, then it must be *them* God was sending him to witness to!

He shared with us how his passion and boldness play out in real
situations:

On one occasion he arrived in a rural village just as the funeral
procession for one of the village leaders was beginning. Seeing an
opportunity, Ragimov struck up a conversation with the two mullahs
(scholars of Islamic teaching) who were to preside over the funeral.
He asked them what they thought had happened to the deceased
man after he took his final breath.

The mullahs could not provide him with a definitive answer.

"Why are you even here if you don't know the answers to these
important questions?" Ragimov challenged them.

"If you're so clever," one of the mullahs replied, "why don't you
speak at the funeral?"

This was an opportunity the pastor couldn't pass up! He walked forward and took a position beside the coffin holding the body of the dead Muslim. He spoke about the hope of eternity in the presence of God through Jesus Christ. His audience listened carefully; the one hundred and fifty people included the two mullahs as well as the village policeman.

Following the end of the funeral service, many of the villagers came forward to speak with Ragimov. They kissed him on both cheeks, a sign of acceptance and respect in their culture.

"This mullah is better than any other that we've heard," they told the Muslim mullahs. "We'd like him to return to our village."

Ragimov was happy to honor their request; he went back later and showed the *JESUS* film.

That was one of his happy-ending stories; a warm welcome and an open door for the gospel.

But there were other stories with much different endings. In one village, just a few months before our conversation, the welcome wasn't nearly as warm. Ragimov traveled to the rural village to visit a family there. When he left, the secret police barged into the family's home, copied the IDs of everyone in the family, and told them the next time Ragimov came for a visit they'd better call police immediately. In fact, they were told, it would be much better and safer if they would not socialize or cooperate with any Christians.

Neither the family nor Pastor Ragimov were intimidated. He was making plans, when we spoke, to return to the village.

He remembers the beatings, pain, and suffering he's endured. But he remembers also the hope he felt when he discovered the truth of the gospel message, that God would send His own Son as a ransom for the people of central Asia and everywhere else.

The joy Ragimov feels in seeing his countrymen hear that message for the first time, and the light in their eyes as they understand the promise of God's love and eternity with Christ, is worth far more than the temporary suffering or tears of a physical beating.

FOR REFLECTION

How can we always be prepared to make a defense to anyone and see every situation as an opportunity to share the gospel? Ragimov isn't the first believer I've met in a hostile or restricted nation that sees funerals as great gospel opportunities. I remember a pastor in China who told me he loves preaching funerals, because people are naturally thinking about eternity, and because the police almost never bother a funeral.

Do you believe, the same way Pastor Ragimov does, that every person you meet has been brought into your path for you to impact that person with the gospel? How would such a mindset affect your actions and conversations? Set a reminder on your phone to pray every day that God will open a door, that day, for you to talk about Jesus' love with someone He places in your path.

PRAYER

Lord, help me see each person I meet through Your eyes, and see every encounter and every conversation as a chance to speak grace and gospel truth into the life of a person You love and You died for.

For Your Journal

_____

_____

_____

_____

_____

_____

_____

_____

_____

_____

_____

_____

From My Journal

The plane ride was an adventure.

I sat right by the emergency exit, and as we sat on the runway, it sounded like air was coming in! [My coworker] asked if the door was closed good, and the stewardess assured us it was. Then, as we took off, the panel that covers the latch fell open—gave me a good scare! The plane is at least twenty years old and decorated in avocado green, paint-flecked yucky yellow, with faded blue seats.

The seats fold forward, too, so if no one's in a seat and the pilot hits the brakes, it folds forward. Fun! Oh yeah—and I could smell gas!

Once we took off, with me praying feverishly, I relaxed and actually took a nap.

DAY 28

"USE THAT FOR TOILET PAPER"

And Agrippa said to Paul, "In a short time would you persuade me to be a Christian?" And Paul said, "Whether short or long, I would to God that not only you but also all who hear me this day might become such as I am—except for these chains."

ACTS 26:28–29

....

Central Asia, 2002

Many of the Christians I meet have amazing BC (before Christ) stories. When I met Telman, he had been sent as a missionary to an isolated part of his central Asian country, a place where there was no church presence. But his BC story fascinated me also.

Telman, BC, was a criminal, raised in a family of criminals. He'd served prison time—well-deserved, he said—for his crimes. His brothers were also criminals.

I asked Telman how a Muslim from a family of criminals would come to be a follower of Jesus Christ.

"The Holy Spirit must touch them," he said. "There is no other way."

It was a warm day, and we sat outside as Telman told me his story. There was a fountain in the city square nearby. Perhaps it was the pleasant surroundings that kept Telman from telling me the unpleasant parts of his conversion story. He told me about his life of crime. And he told me about the ministry that he was doing now, and some of the challenges to that ministry, but he didn't mention the conversion point and the trouble it involved. That part of the story I heard from another Christian, a friend of Telman's.

When Telman, the nominally Muslim criminal, became a follower of Jesus, his family was enraged by his "betrayal." He'd brought shame on the entire family, and someone needed to be punished. But it couldn't have been Telman's idea to leave Islam. He must have been led astray—and Telman's family blamed his wife for his poor choices.

Telman's two brothers beat his wife to punish her.

As a husband, I could only imagine the heartbreak and shame Telman must have felt. Shouldn't a husband protect his wife? If there was anger in his family, shouldn't they have taken it out on him, instead of beating his wife? I could understand why I'd heard that part of the story from someone else rather than directly from Telman. It would be a difficult story for a husband to share.

The persecution they faced didn't deter Telman or his wife. In fact, it only strengthened their resolve to follow the path God had called them to. He began a Bible training course through his church and eventually was commissioned as a missionary to another part of his country. He and his wife packed up and moved, staying at first with some of her relatives as they began the work of planting the gospel flag in that community.

However, the authorities there didn't want a church in their town. Telman was called into the police station, interrogated, and harassed.

He was told that he didn't have government registration to operate a church there. Eventually, his residency documents were withdrawn. He was ordered to leave the city and return to the capital, where he had lived before.

Telman and his wife faced persecution when he chose to follow Christ, and he hadn't given up. He wasn't going to give up his church-planting efforts over a dose of persecution, either.

Back in the capital city, he spoke with his pastor. The church in the capital city did have government registration, so the pastor filed paperwork for Telman's mission ministry to be a sub-ministry of their registered church.

Telman returned to the city and continued gospel meetings there. Once again, he was taken to the police station. Sitting before the chief of police, Telman pulled out the official documents that said his nation's government had approved his work there.

The police chief just smirked. "You can take those papers and use them for toilet paper," he said. "I am the law here."

Telman was kicked out of the city again. Yet again, he was not deterred from the work God had called him to. If he wouldn't be allowed to live in the city, he would simply have to visit the city—often.

He began traveling there—hours in a car, or even more hours on a bus—every week. The group of Christians there was growing as Telman reached out with the gospel. Many who'd heard about him were curious to talk with him. *Is he crazy? Why would he keep coming back after officials made it so clear that he wasn't welcome? What changed him from being jailed for being a criminal to now being interrogated by police for trying to start a church? What is it about his message that makes the authorities so nervous?*

He asked us to pray for his continued ministry, and that many more Muslims in that city would come to know Christ as Savior and King. He was also praying God would allow him to be granted a residency permit, so he and his wife could move there full-time to be closer to the ministry God had called them to, a ministry that God was clearly blessing.

FOR REFLECTION

When God calls you to do something, how easily do you become deterred by opposition? How quickly do you give up if things don't go smoothly from the first moment you start a ministry endeavor?

Telman was told he didn't have permission to operate in a new city. So he got the necessary paperwork. Then he was told his paperwork was useless. But he continued the work. He moved there. Then was told he couldn't live there. But he continued the work by making regular visits. None of the obstacles thrown in front of him stopped him from answering God's call to that city.

Do you have the same resolve? Are you ready to pray and work and strategize your way over, around, or through any obstacle that comes between you and fulfilling the call of God in your life? For your journal, write about an obstacle you're currently facing in your spiritual life. List three ideas how you might overcome it.

Prayer

Lord Jesus, help me boldly continue to do what I sense You are asking me to do, regardless of opposition, inconvenience, or challenges that arise. Give me creative ideas to overcome the challenge I'm currently facing.

For Your Journal

_____

_____

_____

_____

_____

_____

_____

_____

_____

_____

_____

From My Journal

[First day of the trip:] I was about twenty-eight hours in transit here, including a long six-hour layover in London. Got in around midnight last night and to bed around two. Then, of course, I couldn't sleep very well. So I think I got around three hours.

We left the hotel a little after eight a.m. and didn't return until one-thirty a.m.—seventeen and a half hours—but I felt quite good all day long. PTL! We also drove eleven hundred KM [more than six hundred fifty miles] in that time. Our host said I was a hero—said any other foreigner would have been crying after just one hundred KM!

QUOTES TO CONSIDER

Whenever the Church has been thoroughly distinct from the world, she has always prospered. During the first three centuries the world hated the Church. The prison, the stake, the heels of the wild horse, these were thought too good for the followers of Christ. When a man became a Christian, he gave up father and mother, house and lands, nay, his own life also. . . . But then was the age of heroes; that was the time of giants. Never did the Church so much prosper and so truly thrive as when she was baptized in blood. The ship of the Church never sails so gloriously along as when the bloody spray of her martyrs falls upon her deck. We *must* suffer, and we *must* die, if we are ever to conquer this world for Christ.

—Charles Spurgeon[6]

You then, my child, be strengthened by the grace that is in Christ Jesus, and what you have heard from me in the presence of many witnesses entrust to faithful men, who will be able to teach others also. Share in suffering as a good soldier of Christ Jesus.

2 Timothy 2:1–3

ЗАЛЫМА ДУШМӘН КӘСИЛ..?

DAY 29

"NO ONE WILL STOP THE GOSPEL"

I charge you in the presence of God and of Christ Jesus, who is to judge the living and the dead, and by his appearing and his kingdom: preach the word; be ready in season and out of season; reprove, rebuke, and exhort, with complete patience and teaching.

2 TIMOTHY 4:1–2

....

Azerbaijan, 2002

Before Pastor Yalov became a fervent Christian and bold evangelist, he was a passionate Muslim—more fervent in following Muhammed than most men in his nation. He was well-educated and well-off financially, yet never seemed to find true peace.

Being a devout Muslim, he read the Quran to find answers to the questions his heart kept asking. He also fulfilled one of his Islamic obligations by making the pilgrimage to Mecca, the *Hajj*. He was doing everything his religion taught him to do, yet still lacked peace in his heart. Despondent, he began preparing to take his own life.

"I tried to live my life by the *Shariah* Law," he told me and a coworker during a visit to Azerbaijan's capital city. "I felt something was not enough in my life. In the Quran, I found no answers for my questions. I thought I was stupid, that I didn't have enough knowledge in my head. So I read more and more. But as I read, I had *more* questions."

A pastor invited Yalov to join in a Christian meeting where there were six Azeri believers. Yalov was the seventh man in the group, the only one not already committed to following Christ. For six months, Yalov attended the group's meetings and read the Bible. The pastor told him about Jesus and the opportunity to know for sure what would happen after he died. Yalov continued to read the Quran also, comparing the words of Muhammed to the words of Jesus.

One day, as he opened his Bible, his eyes fell onto the words of Psalm 91:14: "I will deliver him; I will set him on high, because *he has known My name*" (NKJV, emphasis added).

"I need to call out to God," Yalov thought in a seeking prayer. "But I don't know what His name is." God heard his prayer, and after six months of being the only non-believer in his Bible study group, the Bible verses he'd been reading and the things the pastor had told him finally clicked in his heart and mind. Yalov committed his life to Christ. Now the group was seven Christians reading the Bible together.

The change in Yalov was immediate and dramatic; seeing the difference Jesus made in the life of her husband, Yalov's wife soon also followed Jesus. But not everyone in the family was so pleased with Yalov's choice. His own mother expelled him from the family home, saying that by leaving Islam he'd brought shame on himself and all his relatives.

For more than two years after that, Yalov slept in his office. He would pull two desks together every night to form a makeshift bed. He sought further training in the gospel and in following Jesus; he wanted to lead not only his own family to Christ but also his countrymen. He was discipled and sent out for ministry.

Such ministry is costly in a Muslim nation. Soon, Yalov was arrested, along with another believer who had joined him. They were held fifteen days, interrogated, and pressured to return to Islam and stop their evangelism work.

The following year, he was arrested again, along with another pastor, right in the middle of leading a worship service. They were held eight days in underground solitary confinement cells. The cell was three feet wide and only five feet long; not even enough room to lay straight on the floor.

There was a small window in the door of the cell for guards to watch the prisoners. Yalov, though, perhaps remembering Paul's instruction to Timothy to "be ready in season and out of season," assumed the window had been left there so he and his coworker could preach to the guards. Yalov and the other pastor took turns.

One of the guards was complaining of severe stomach pain. Yalov, through the small window in the door of his cell, prayed Jesus would heal the man's stomach. Immediately, the guard began to feel better as Yalov's prayers were being answered.

"The guards knew that we were not criminals," Yalov told me. He and the other pastor asked the guards to bring them a copy of the *JESUS* film. The guards agreed not only to bring a copy of the movie, but also to allow the two pastors to show the film to other prisoners!

"We showed the *JESUS* film right there in the prison," Yalov said. "Many of the guards accepted Jesus."

Their "cell church" kept growing. Ten inmates chose to follow Christ and accept His offer of forgiveness. When I met Yalov, after his release from prison, three of those former inmates had been released. They were now members of his church.

As our time together was coming to an end, I asked my new

friend if he thought he would be arrested again. It seemed odd to me when he answered the question, smiling broadly.

"I would be very willing to be arrested again," he said. "Anyone who arrests me will hear the Word of God. It will be another opportunity to preach the gospel. No matter what happens to me, millions of people will preach the gospel. It is too late to stop it. No one will stop the gospel!"

FOR REFLECTION

What are the "windows" in your life through which others may be watching you? Perhaps they exist in your workplace, in your neighborhood, or among the other parents at your kids' school. For your journal, write down ways each of those "windows" can give you opportunities to preach the gospel and share Jesus' love with others. Are you willing to endure inconvenience, even difficulty, if it means more opportunities to introduce people to Christ?

PRAYER

Lord, thank You for the boldness of my brother, Yalov, to say, "Anyone who arrests me will hear the Word of God." Help me to be equally bold to say, "Anyone who works with me . . . anyone whose kids are in the same class as mine . . . anyone God puts in my pathway . . . *will hear* the Word of God."

For Your Journal

_____

_____

_____

_____

_____

_____

_____

From My Journal

The good news is that there is a new hotel in [city we are in to meet with local Christians].

The bad news is that we aren't in it.

The new hotel is outside the city, and [a coworker] thought for our purposes it wasn't good. You might have to wait an hour for a taxi to come by.

So we are in a downtown hotel that makes the [last hotel we stayed at] look like the lap of luxury!

No toilet paper. No toilet seats. No sheets. Running water only seven hours a day—and a strange, sulfurous smell when the water does run.

If we get our meetings here taken care of tonight, I might push for the new hotel tomorrow night. Right now, the thought of two nights here is maybe more than I can handle.

They did just move us to a "suite" that has A/C . . .but otherwise isn't much better. I am seriously missing home about now.

DAY 30

"IN THE STEPS OF THE APOSTLES"

For to this you have been called, because Christ also suffered for you, leaving you an example, so that you might follow in his steps.

1 PETER 2:21

....

China, Early 2000s

When you visit Christians in China, it doesn't take long to learn that the picture of religious freedom that the government works hard to portray to outsiders isn't accurate. On one trip, I was given a free copy in my hotel of a magazine, *Beijing Review*. The cover photo was of a woman in an obvious church choir robe, with a cross on the front. The cover headline was "Guaranteed Freedom," in all caps, with a subhead that said "All the religious affairs are run independently by the religious groups."

"Daniel," who came to meet with us late one night via a circuitous route designed to ensure he wasn't being followed, told us a different story about "all the religious affairs."

Daniel is a leader in a large, unregistered church. He often serves as a right-hand man for the pastor, a man who spent many years in prison for his ministry. And, of course, the Public Security Bureau knows exactly who Daniel is.

"My neighbor's phone line is very clear, and always working," he told us. "My phone line is cut often, and I hear a noise on the line." It might make many of us nervous to know we were constantly being watched, that every conversation was being listened to. Daniel sees it a little differently: if there are people listening, then he has an opportunity to witness for Christ.

"It is not only the government that is watching," he says, "but also fellow citizens who are unbelievers." Because of this, he consciously chooses to live out his witness of Christ's love and forgiveness.

Daniel exudes an unruffled calmness and a rock-solid faith in Christ. His words are measured out carefully; it seems he doesn't want to waste even one. He's comfortable in the pauses between words in our conversation. He seems, to me, to be a man who could sit in a police interrogation room without even a minor uptick in his pulse rate. We've just met, but I already feel both friendship and admiration for this man of God.

What would happen, we asked Daniel, if he were caught meeting with foreign Christians—people like us?

"Well, you would be sent out of China and blacklisted so that you could not come back."

"Yes, but what would happen to *you?*"

"It hasn't happened yet, but I am fully prepared, like Paul says [in Acts 21:12–13] to go to Jerusalem, and even to death."

To an unbeliever, that might sound fatalistic or negative, but Daniel sees it very differently. "Difficulty and persecution is a kind of blessing," he told us. "Persecution and difficulties make a Christian strong and mature. The early church in the first century was not like things in the United Kingdom or the United States [today]. It was more like Pakistan, Afghanistan, China, and North Korea.

"We always say, 'Follow in the steps of the apostles.' Where are their steps? In difficulties. In persecution."

In the year before our conversation, the church Daniel served had baptized four hundred and fifty new believers. It's difficult to keep secret a church growing that fast. The reason for their growth is simple: faithful Christians sharing the good news from person to person. They don't consider evangelism to be the pastor's job, or the church leader's job. They consider every believer in Christ an evangelist.

Our time with Daniel is coming to a close. He will leave first, checking his surroundings carefully as he begins a circuitous journey back to his home. We will wait a while before leaving, drink another cup of tea, just in case someone is watching the exit.

I asked Daniel how he was getting ready, in case he was arrested for his gospel work.

"Most important is spiritual preparation," he said. "For example, read more Bible every day, and memorize more and more each day. I can manage someday if I have no Bible."

"Do you expect that to happen?" I asked him. "Do you expect to be arrested?"

"If that is God's will," he answered calmly, "I will follow it. All authority is given to Jesus, and He has commanded us to make disciples. But I don't think we are alone or lonely. Like Nehemiah says [4:20] the battle is not ours. The battle is the Lord's. It's not 'we fight' or 'we will fight for ourselves.' No, no, no. *God will fight for us.*"

He puts on his coat, and we say our goodbyes. He heads into the dark, chilly night, back onto the path God has called him to walk, "in the steps of the apostles."

FOR REFLECTION

When we think of following "in the steps of the apostles," most of us probably imagine times sitting around the fire with Jesus, seeing thousands come to faith in the Messiah at Pentecost, or seeing the sick healed and the lame walk in the name of Jesus. There aren't nearly as many warm, fuzzy feelings when we think about being locked in the stocks in the long, cold hours after midnight at the Philippian jail, the beatings, the shipwrecks, or being crucified upside down. But the apostles' footprints go through these experiences, too. Their path traverses both mountaintops of faith and wonder, and valleys of darkness, pain, and doubt.

Are you following in the steps of the apostles today? Does today's path lead you along the mountaintop, or through the valley? Most importantly, regardless of where you are on the path, are you walking faithfully?

PRAYER

Lord, help me to be ready to serve You, whether the path of Your will lies in comfort and ease or in suffering and pain. Help me walk faithfully "in the path of the apostles," both when it is easy and when it is difficult and painful. Allow those watching how I live my life to see You in me.

For Your Journal

_____

_____

_____

_____

_____

_____

_____

_____

_____

_____

From My Journal

Daniel told us that he is prepared to suffer for his faith. He has chosen to prepare himself for that day. That theme is something we've run into at every stop on this trip . . . the idea that these believers were ready for suffering because they got ready. They knew the day would come, and they prepared. I wonder if that's the message of this trip—get ready!

DAY 31

"I WILL GIVE YOU REST"

AFROOZ, PART 1

"Come to me, all who labor and are heavy laden, and I will give
you rest."

MATTHEW 11:28

....

Turkey, 2003

My coworker and I met Afrooz at a church in Turkey, where she'd
fled as a refugee from her native Iran. After coming to faith in Christ
in Iran, she and her husband ministered to others boldly. But when
the government began threatening to take away their daughter, they
fled the country, seeking safety and asylum somewhere else.

Afrooz had found Jesus when she wasn't even looking for Him,
and her life would never be the same. In spite of having fled her
homeland, in spite of not knowing where her family would end up
or when they'd find a permanent home, Afrooz had a quiet, calm
assurance that I found myself drawn to. She'd found peace in the

midst of the storm. His name is Jesus.

We sat in a back room at the church, a center for helping refugees. There were people hustling around, working on food prep and meeting other needs. We sipped tea and listened to Afrooz share her story:

I was studying, going to college, and working. I was under pressure, and my mother and father weren't with me, so I was lonely. Therefore, I prayed to Allah to help me relax and that the pressure would go away.

I tried my best (as a Muslim). I followed the religious orders of Islam. I did my best to get as deep as possible, gaining access to Allah as much as possible. But actually, the stress was growing, and the mental pressure was beating me up and absorbing all of my energy. At my job, they sent me to another company to work in another place for a month, so I had more problems and more work to do in addition to my studies.

One night, in my room, I talked to Allah, and complained: "How much pressure? This is enough! How much can I stand? I am working and studying. Why aren't you helping me? Why aren't you giving me relief?"

I threatened, "If you are going to help me, tonight you should show yourself to me. If you don't show me a sign tonight, then I will turn to this material life and I will be a sinner." So after I finished, I said, "I will be staying up all night and waiting for your sign so I can see and believe that you are here with me."

I was talking to the god of Muhammed. I was expecting to see Allah. I complained for an hour. I got tired, so I put my head on my prayer mat. It was midnight. I saw a light coming into my room and spreading. I was frightened and ran out of the room. Then I told myself, "Didn't I ask for something?" So I convinced myself that I should go back and sit in the prayer place and see what would happen.

The room was full of light. I thought it was morning, but later, I realized it was midnight. I lifted my head and was seeing Jesus Christ.

He was wearing white. While I had never seen a picture of the Messiah, I recognized that this could only be the Messiah.

I liked to write poems, so I always had a paper and pen ready for things that would come to my mind. Immediately, at that time, I started to take notes.

I wrote [in Farsi], *"Come to me, all you who labor and are heavy laden, and I will give you rest."*

I actually got a little bit angry at this. I was looking for Muhammed's god, and Jesus the Messiah comes to me?! What is this?! So I closed up the prayer mat and said, "I am done with this! I'm going to sleep!"

The next night, I dreamed and saw the Messiah. He said, "Didn't I tell you to come under My shadow and come with Me and be safe?" So I was telling myself, "This is the Messiah coming to me. Is this the real God? I should be seeing Allah or Muhammed."

One of my colleagues [at her workplace] *noticed I was upset and asked, "Is something wrong with you?"*

I said, "Well, my mother is in America, and I haven't seen her in a while. I don't know if I'll ever be able to see her again. That is what's bothering me."

He started calming me down, saying: "God is always with you. God is love. Bring your complaints to Him." Usually in Iran, people working in a company don't come up to you and say, "I'm a Christian." After I was there for three weeks, he came up to me and told me he was a Christian. So when he was talking to me about God's love, I started to complain. "What kind of God would allow me to feel this way, to have this kind of pressure?"

Afrooz pulled out the notebook that she carried with her every-where, and showed her new friend the words she'd written in her room the night of the vision: "Come to me, all you who labor and are heavy laden, and I will give you rest."

Her coworker pulled out a book of his own, carefully going through the pages until he found the one he was looking for. He held it out to Afrooz, pointing to a particular spot on the page.

Afrooz looked, and the words in this book (Matt. 11:28) were the same words she'd written down in her notebook.

"What book is this?" she demanded. It was the first Bible she'd ever seen. Her friend told her what it was and even offered to get one for her.

"That," Afrooz told us, "was the beginning of my faith."

It was the first step on a long road. And the road would not be an easy one.

FOR REFLECTION

Perhaps you see yourself in Afrooz's story, crying out to God, "Show Yourself to me! I'm desperate!" If that is the case: take courage, my friend. God answers prayer, and He does show Himself real and powerful in our lives.

But maybe you're not in a place of desperation right now, and that prayer seems far from you. If that's the case, perhaps you're the Christian coworker in this story. If God allows you to see a need around you, are you ready to open His Word and speak peace and hope into that desperate soul? Are you ready to point your coworker, friend, or neighbor to the One who can truly bring rest? For your journal, write whether you are in the position of desperately seeking or in the position to help someone who is. What does it mean to you, whichever place you are in, that Jesus offers to "give you rest"?

PRAYER

Lord Jesus, I want to experience You this week! I want to see Your hand at work in my life. Fill me anew; give rest and peace

in place of weariness and struggle. Allow me to speak Your
peace to those around me anxious to hear.

For Your Journal

_____

_____

_____

_____

_____

_____

_____

_____

_____

_____

_____

From My Journal

When Afrooz showed him the words she had written
down, he showed them to her in the Bible. She was saved
shortly thereafter!

Isn't that AMAZING?! Where missionaries can't go, and
where a Bible is so hard to get, God is appearing Himself in
dreams and visions!

PRAYING FOR PERSECUTED CHRISTIANS

Afrooz's story of a personal encounter with Jesus is not an unusual one in the Muslim world. In fact, I've had gospel workers tell me when they first meet a Muslim they often ask, "Have you had any strange dreams lately?"

Muslims already believe there is one god. They already believe god should be obeyed. So they are ready to follow when they have an encounter where Jesus demonstrates that He is God.

PRAY TODAY for God's Spirit to move in powerful ways—in Muslim nations and around the world. Pray that people—Muslims, Hindus, atheists, Buddhists, and others—will have supernatural encounters with Jesus Christ and His mighty power, will be drawn to His Word, and will understand their need for a Savior.

DAY 32

PROVE YOU ARE CHRISTIANS

AFROOZ, PART 2

"What therefore God has joined together, let not man separate."
MARK 10:9

....

Turkey, 2003

Afrooz's faith began when Jesus appeared to her late one night in her room in her native Iran, promising He could give rest to her and all who "are weary and heavy laden." Afrooz found spiritual rest in the Savior. But her earthly life in the *Islamic Republic* of Iran actually became much more difficult after leaving Allah to follow Jesus.

When she tried to find a new job, Afrooz found that no employer would hire her once it became known she was no longer a Muslim and was now a Christian. Iran's government, she told me, makes trouble for companies that hire "apostates," so even if she was offered a job, it was at a lower-than-normal pay rate, and with no benefits. But trying to find a job was just the introduction to persecution for Afrooz.

Through her church, she met a Christian man. The two decided to get married. They held their wedding ceremony in a church, but that decision brought on them the wrath of the secret police.

Police barged into their hotel room on their wedding night and arrested both Afrooz and her husband. "How do we even know you are married?" they asked, since the couple didn't have documentation from their local mosque registering their nuptials.

"What I'm wearing says I'm a bride," Afrooz shot back. "And what he's wearing says he's a groom!" The police weren't satisfied. They demanded to know where the wedding had taken place, and the name of the clergy who had presided. When they learned the identity of Afrooz's pastor, they threatened him with arrest as well.

The couple was eventually released, and decided to move to a different part of Iran where they wouldn't be known as apostates. Hopefully the pressure against them would be less. But even in this "safe" place, they were threatened by radical Muslims who somehow knew they had left Islam to follow Christ.

After their daughter was born, Afrooz and her husband faced further danger and threats. They named their daughter Emmanuel, a Christian name. But when they went to register for her birth certificate, officials demanded "proof" that it was in fact a Christian name. And further, "We need documents to prove that *you* are Christians."

Apostasy can be a capital offense in Iran. Documents that "proved" Afrooz and her husband had left Islam would also be "proof" they deserved to be executed. And even if they wanted such documents, what mosque would issue them? It's easy to get documentation that you've changed from another religion to Islam, but nearly impossible to get any paperwork saying you've left the Islamic faith.

Afrooz and her husband prayed God would move in their situation, and they continued to minister within their church. Afrooz became a leader among women in the church, and even traveled to other parts of Iran to minister. But the government had not forgotten their apostasy.

When it came time for Emmanuel to attend preschool, the school refused to certify her attendance, or give the documentation she would need to begin elementary school. Afrooz knew what could happen: the government would say she and her husband were not providing for their daughter's education. They could declare them unfit parents and take Emmanuel away.

Afrooz and her husband had made peace with the fact that following Christ in Iran might lead them to prison. But the thought of losing their daughter, her being taken away and raised as a Muslim, weighed heavily upon them.

After much prayer and heart searching, they decided they couldn't risk having Emmanuel taken away. They fled the country, first to Turkey (where I met and interviewed her) and eventually to a western nation.

Several years after meeting Afrooz in Turkey, I received an email from her. She'd heard a radio interview I'd done that aired on a Christian station in the city she now calls home. Was I the same Todd that met her at the church in Istanbul? It was wonderful to hear how God was still using her and her family, and to hear that they were safe.

Afrooz continues to minister for Christ in her new homeland, including sharing her story with women's groups and challenging believers to live wholeheartedly for Christ.

FOR REFLECTION

Sometimes God calls us to stand for Him in the face of persecution or hardship, even at the risk or in the midst of great suffering. Other times, He directs us to leave, to let the pressure die down or even to escape the hardship. The apostle Paul was lowered in a basket to escape Damascus and those seeking to take his life. That same Paul also appealed to Caesar and demanded the right to defend himself and his faith before the highest authority. God directed him in different ways at different junctures of his ministry life.

Are you more prone to stand boldly in the face of opposition, or to look for a way to avoid confrontation? Has there been a time God directed you to take a bold stand in the face of those opposed to the gospel message, or even in the face of persecution? Has there been another time you've sensed His leading for you to escape, lay low, or avoid direct confrontation? As you look back, do you see the wisdom of His leading? What were the kingdom results? Write about it for your journal.

PRAYER

Lord Jesus, help me clearly hear Your voice and see Your plans for me. Give me courage and boldness in times You call me to stand firm; give me wisdom and grace in times You direct me to move or step back. And, in every situation, allow me to be a blessing to others in Your name.

For Your Journal

From My Journal

After that, we met with an Iranian Christian that [name withheld] had told us about—and sent ten Farsi Bibles for. He came to our hotel, and we talked for a few minutes, then rushed him away, because we don't trust the hotel people here—they seem just a bit TOO interested in our comings and goings and who we are talking to. . . .

The hotel people looked at us really strangely when we brought [Christians we were meeting with] back to our room. I don't know what they think but they give us the creeps—seem to be watching closely. I wonder whether my phone call was listened in on. I couldn't get a sat-phone signal [which would have bypassed anyone's ability to listen in].

DAY 33

"EVEN THE QURAN SAYS JESUS IS COMING"

Everyone who believes that Jesus is the Christ has been born of God, and everyone who loves the Father loves whoever has been born of him. By this we know that we love the children of God, when we love God and obey his commandments. For this is the love of God, that we keep his commandments. And his commandments are not burdensome.

1 JOHN 5:1–3

....

Bangladesh, 2005

When I met Hasem Sharkar, he was forty-five years old and had been following Jesus only six months. Already, in those few months, his faith had cost him his home and his job. But he wasn't about to slow down or turn away.

Sharkar is an illiterate man who worked as a day laborer in the village where he lived. He was born into a Muslim family, and he'd followed the teachings of his parents and others in his village all his life.

Then, an evangelist came to Sharkar's village and showed the *JESUS* film. Sharkar watched the film very carefully. He understood from Islamic teachings that Jesus was a prophet, but the Jesus he saw on screen was much *more* than just a messenger from God. Sharkar had many questions for the evangelist. As they spoke and he considered what he'd seen on the film, Sharkar was convinced Jesus was the Son of God. Jesus provided answers Muhammed couldn't.

"I love Him," Sharkar explained, "because Jesus is the only Savior. I understand that, and I accepted Jesus. I love this gift!"

As a day laborer, Sharkar would show up in the center of the village every day to see which land owners or businessmen needed workers that day. But when word got around that Sharkar was no longer a Muslim, but an apostate infidel, he was no longer offered work in the morning. His income quickly dried up.

Yet Sharkar wasn't swayed by the pressure, or silenced by the persecution. In fact, he couldn't keep quiet about Jesus. Just a few weeks after coming to faith himself, Sharkar invited some young men from his village to go with him to a Christian service in a nearby village. The men went along, heard the message, and they too decided to follow Jesus.

Now Sharkar wasn't just an apostate; he was also a missionary causing other Muslims to fall away from their faith. It was no longer enough to shun him. Now he must be punished.

Angry villagers confronted Sharkar, and angry shouts quickly became angry fists. Sharkar was beaten; his entire face was swollen and bruised after the beating.

The man who couldn't read saw his persecution as a test from above. "I have given my life to Jesus," he told me, "so this is kind of a test to see if I am a true believer or not."

He passed the test. In the six months he'd been following Jesus, Sharkar had led thirty Muslims to faith in Christ. Part of his message to them was drawn from the teachings of Islam he'd learned from his boyhood. "Even the Quran says Jesus is coming!" he said excitedly. "It says He'll lead the last Friday prayers. They know! This is the teaching of Islam!"

When I met him, he was living in a safe haven that VOM sponsored for Christians who'd been kicked out by their families or villages in Bangladesh. They started with chapel every morning at five-thirty, and Sharkar was soaking up the discipleship and evangelism training. Without the ability to read, Sharkar's Bible study was all done by audio: he had the four gospels on cassette tapes, and a hand-crank cassette player where he can turn the crank and listen to the Scriptures.

Shortly after coming home from Bangladesh, I came across a passage from Oswald Chambers that made me think of Sharkar:

> We tend to say that because a person has natural ability, he will make a good Christian. It is not a matter of our equipment, but a matter of our poverty; not of what we bring with us, but of what God puts into us. The only thing of value is being taken into the compelling purpose of God and being made His friends. God's friendship is with people who know their poverty. As Christians we are not here for our own purpose at all—we are here for the purpose of God, and the two are not the same.[7]

Reading this passage, and thinking of the people I'd met in Bangladesh, I found myself deeply challenged by Sharkar's testimony. When we think of "natural ability," Sharkar probably wouldn't make the top half of our list. He can't read, and he's been a Christian for only six months. But when it comes to fulfilling "the purpose of God," Sharkar is a first-round draft pick! In the six months he's walked with Jesus, he's already been in trouble—beaten!—because he won't stop telling people about Jesus! He's already led thirty Muslims to Christ!

The excuses I might make, or my own laziness, seem pretty pitiful in light of the courage, passion for Christ, and go-get-'em witnessing spirit of a bold believer like Sharkar.

FOR REFLECTION

What does Sharkar's story say to you? Are you relying on "natural ability" to serve Christ, or are you allowing Him to empower and send you out as He sees fit to best fulfill His purposes? Ask God to show you areas where you're counting on your own abilities instead of "what God puts into us." Journal or discuss with a Christian friend how to rely more fully on Christ and less on yourself.

PRAYER

Jesus, thank You for the example of my brother Sharkar. Help me also have a passion to serve You and tell others about You, with whatever talents, skills, and understanding You give me. I commit myself again to Your purpose, which is greater and higher than my own. Amen.

For Your Journal

_____

_____

_____

_____

_____

_____

_____

_____

_____

_____

From My Journal

I'm lying on my bed, under the mosquito net, getting ready to fall asleep.

We drove five hours from Dhaka today, including a ferry ride across a wide, WIDE river. And this is the dry season! Then we parked, crossed another river in a canoe, then walked a quarter mile to the compound here.

This is, distance, technology, and culturally, about as far from Oklahoma as you can get!

QUOTES TO CONSIDER

Though we do not have much of it in this age of spineless religion, there is nevertheless much in the Bible about the place of moral determination in the service of the Lord. The Old Testament tells us that "Jacob vowed a vow," and Daniel "purposed in his heart." Paul determined "not to know anything among you, save Jesus Christ, and Him crucified." Above all, we have the example of the Lord Jesus "setting His face like a flint" and walking straight toward the Cross. These and many others have left us a record of spiritual greatness born out of a will firmly set to do the will of God! They did not try to float to heaven on a perfumed cloud, but cheerfully accepted the fact that "with purpose of heart they must cleave to the Lord." We must surrender—and in that terrible, wonderful moment we may feel that our will has been forever broken, but such is not the case. In His conquest of the soul, God purges the will and brings it into union with His own, but He never breaks it!

—A. W. Tozer[8]

And when they had called in the apostles, they beat them and charged them not to speak in the name of Jesus, and let them go. Then they left the presence of the council, rejoicing that they were counted worthy to suffer dishonor for the name.

Acts 5:40–41

TORTURED HANDS —PART 1

How then will they call on him in whom they have not believed? And how are they to believe in him of whom they have never heard? And how are they to hear without someone preaching? And how are they to preach unless they are sent? As it is written, "How beautiful are the feet of those who preach the good news!"

ROMANS 10:14–15

....

Seoul, Korea, 2008

I will never forget Mrs. Choi's hands—or her tears.

We met "Choi Yong Jin" in Seoul, South Korea. But she was brought up north of the DMZ in the Democratic People's Republic of Korea, the Hermit Kingdom that is completely closed off from the rest of the world.

To understand the persecution of Christians in North Korea, you must understand a little bit about *Juche*, the so-called ideology of the North Korean regime that is, in reality, the required religion of every North Korean citizen. *Juche* ("self-reliance") teaches that members of the Kim family that dominate the country's government are in fact divine beings.

Children are taught to say "grace" before they eat: "Thank you, Father Kim Il Sung, for our food." Every North Korean is taught "hymns" of praises to the Kims from the national hymnal, which contains six hundred such songs.

So when a person follows Jesus, it is not simply a matter of following a different religion, or even of following a "Western" idea. To believe Jesus is Lord is to believe that Kim Il Sung is not Lord—and that is treason. And North Korea's government relentlessly hunts the treasonous, especially those with the audacity to spread their ideas to others.

Mrs. Choi was married to a powerful Communist official in North Korea—a man with enough authority that one word from him could get someone released from prison. He vouched for a friend of their family, and the man was released from prison. In gratefulness, the man came to their home bearing a thank you gift: a damp, moldy book that had been hidden, buried in the soil.

"This is the story of someone from heaven who helps poor people," the man told Mr. and Mrs. Choi. "Would you like to read it?"

The Chois had never heard of a Bible or Jesus, but the story sounded intriguing, so they accepted the gift. Every night, Mrs. Choi carefully covered the windows of their home to make sure no light got out and no one could see in. In North Korea, neighbors are expected to report any strange happenings at the houses of those living near them. Mrs. Choi wanted to ensure there was nothing to report.

She would then snuggle into a corner of the home and pull a blanket over her head, forming a small tent of privacy in which to read. Then she would light a candle, being careful not to catch the blanket on fire, and begin reading the musty old book.

The man who'd given them the book instructed them to read

five parts of it first before reading the whole thing: the first section, called "Genesis," and then four other sections all written by the same man, whose name was John. He'd told them to read those parts three times before they read the rest of it.

She would read for hours each night before blowing out the candle, coming out from under the blanket and putting the book back in its carefully chosen hiding place. When she would come out, after the reading sessions, her nose was full of black soot from the candle and her mind was full of questions. She was fascinated by the man Jesus as described in John's gospel. "In Him was life," she read in John 1:4. He was the Lamb of God who takes away sin, said John 1:29. John 7:7 said that the world hated Him, and 1 John 3:13 said that the world would hate those who followed Him, too.

But there were good promises in the book too, promises for victory and blessing. "And this is the victory that has overcome the world—our faith," said 1 John 5:4.

The story was so intriguing, Mrs. Choi had many questions. But there was no one to answer. A few months later, she saw a chance to get some answers. Her uncle, who'd left North Korea and now lived in China, came for a visit. As the family sat down to dinner, Choi noticed that before he began eating his rice, her uncle bowed his head for just a moment. As she watched him pray, the Holy Spirit moved in her heart, and the stories she'd been reading snapped into clear focus. Questions faded, and her faith was born.

The next morning, her uncle taught her a song: "Amazing Grace, how sweet the sound that saved a wretch like me!" Later, she was able to get a permit to visit him in China, and while she was there, she went to her first-ever gathering of believers. The pastor of the meeting prayed with her before she crossed back into North Korea.

In a nation where everyone is expected to spy on everyone else, her faith didn't stay a secret for long. Soon Mrs. Choi was arrested, charged with being a "religious spy" and "spreading anti-communist ideas."

The atmosphere in the room shifted as she continued her story. We quietly celebrated and praised God as we listened to her tell how God reached her with the gospel message and saved her. But our hearts—and then our eyes—began to weep as we heard what it cost her to follow Christ.

"I was caught by the police," she told us, "and I was tortured very seriously. They forced me to kneel down on the chair, and they stepped on my knees. They beat my face—and every part of my body. My face was bruised and very black. They asked me to confess my spying acts, and said, 'Tell us about the man who brought the Bibles to you.' I told them I was not a spy, and I did not commit any spying acts against the North Korean government. I did not tell the man's name, and I insisted in telling them that I was the only one who read the Bible."

When the torture didn't produce the results they wanted, the police changed tactics. . . .

FOR REFLECTION

Mrs. Choi and her husband had never seen a Bible and had absolutely no concept of who Jesus was. It's easy to think, *Of course, there are people who have no concept of Jesus in North Korea, but that couldn't be true in the West.* But it could be true here, too. Do you know someone who may have no concept of Jesus or never have seen a Bible? Perhaps it's someone who immigrated to your city from another country. Or it may be someone who has lived here all their life but never been around Christians. Write down some ideas about how you can start a conversation that will introduce them to who Jesus is.

PRAYER

Jesus, please protect me from taking it for granted that the people around me know about You or know Your Word. Help me see opportunities where I can speak Your name and Your truth into the hearts of those who haven't yet heard.

For Your Journal

_____

_____

_____

_____

_____

_____

_____

_____

From My Journal

I had a very embarrassing thing happen today! Apparently, the average Korean man doesn't weigh as much as I weigh, because in the middle of interviewing one of the North Koreans we met today, my plastic chair just sort of disintegrated under me, and I found myself crashing to the floor!

It wasn't like I was leaning back in the chair and tipped over . . . the chair just collapsed! They were very apologetic and quickly got me a new chair . . .but I was mortified.

I guess it's time to start that diet, huh . . . ?

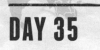

DAY 35

TORTURED HANDS —PART 2

For everyone who has been born of God overcomes the world.
And this is the victory that has overcome the world—our faith.

1 JOHN 5:4

....

Seoul, Korea, 2008

When torturing Mrs. Choi's body didn't convince her to reveal the name of the man who'd delivered the Bible to her, North Korean police changed tactics. They decided to try torturing her heart.

Police went to Mr. Choi, telling him that if he would testify against his wife and admit their "crime" of having and reading a Bible, then she could soon come home and be reunited with him.

Then they went back to Mrs. Choi in jail: "Your husband will be a witness against your crime," they gloated. "So you might as well confess everything."

Recalling the betrayal, even years later, Mrs. Choi could barely continue the story, pausing often to catch her breath and wipe her tears.

"After that, they tied my legs and hung me upside down and beat me. In prison, I was beaten every day, all day long.

"The policemen had me stand up and place my hands out of the door, because there was a small window in the door, and they hit my fingers and my hands with a pipe. I was bleeding all over, and my hands were torn. I could not use my hands for more than twenty days."

She held up her hands to show us as she told the story; the marks of this torture were still clear as several fingers jut out at odd angles. I couldn't imagine the pain of having your fingers beaten with a pipe.

When the time came for Mrs. Choi's trial, her husband realized the police had lied to him. Instead of testifying against his wife, he offered bold words in her defense. Amazingly, at the end of the five-hour trial, she was found "Not Guilty."

But "Not Guilty" was not an acceptable verdict to the regime, and the judge's decision was thrown out and a new trial ordered. Her second trial lasted only an hour, and Mrs. Choi was unable to speak in her own defense because she'd been beaten so badly that her face was too swollen to talk. This time she was found guilty and sentenced to fifteen years in prison.

"I prayed all the time in prison," she told us, "even when I was beaten by the guards."

She also remembered some of the verses she'd read on the musty, moldy pages of that Bible. She remembered Jesus' words, and paraphrased them to us: "Anybody who hit you on the right cheek, turn to them the left cheek also."

She held onto the promises she'd read in 1 John that her faith could overcome the world, and she trusted it was true even of the world created by the Kim regime.

After one year in prison, Mrs. Choi weighed sixty-two pounds. When her husband was allowed to visit, she begged him to *get her out.* He sold their home and collected funds from every friend or family member willing to contribute. He went back to the prison with all the money he'd collected, as well as a television. Paying off the guards worked, and Mrs. Choi was allowed to return home.

"Before this experience," she told us, "I believed, 'My country is the best country in the world!' But I realized in prison what is the reality of North Korea. I told my husband, 'If I can recover my health again, I do not want to live in this land, because I know now what this land is like!'"

Eventually, she did escape, crossing into China and eventually reaching South Korea.

Sometimes when we meet with persecuted Christians, they've worked completely through their feelings about their persecutors and come to a point of love and forgiveness. Mrs. Choi wasn't there yet. In fact, she described her rather elaborate idea of how Kim Jong Il (North Korea's leader at that time) could be punished for the terrible things he'd inflicted on his countrymen. Seeing her tears, and her oddly bent fingers, we certainly understood her anger.

When we met her, Mrs. Choi *was* fighting back against the evil regime that enslaves her homeland, but her fight was not with guns or bombs but spiritual weapons. She was working as part of a Christian radio ministry in Seoul broadcasting Scriptures and other Christian programming across the DMZ into North Korea. One of the ministries of this station is to allow North Korean defectors like Mrs. Choi to share their stories over the air, letting all North Koreans know the truth about their "Dear Leaders," and letting friends and family know she'd made it out alive, was still living, and had reached safety in South Korea.

Her fingers are beaten and battered; her hands will never recover the dexterity and strength they had before they were beaten with a pipe. But her voice is powerful as it speaks of a faith that can overcome the world—even the Hermit Kingdom world now ruled mercilessly by Kim Jong Un.

FOR REFLECTION

Part of the definition of the Greek word translated "overcomes" in 1 John 5:4 is "to conquer, to come out victorious." As Christians, we "overcome the world" when we hold fast to our faith, victorious against temptations and persecutions—even unto death.

Sitting with Mrs. Choi reminded me of the hard work of forgiveness. It'd be nice to think "overcoming" means Jesus magically takes away the consequences of other peoples' sins against us, instantly removing bitterness, anger, and hurt feelings toward those who've wronged us. While some people experience that miraculous power, Mrs. Choi was still working toward a point of forgiveness. Perhaps you're in that place, too. If that's true, be honest—with yourself and with God. Ask Him to soften your heart. Seek His divine power to enable you to "overcome," to completely forgive and lay aside the hurt, anger, or bitterness you feel.

PRAYER

Lord Jesus, thank You for forgiving me for the sins I've committed. Thank You for dying on the cross to pay the price for wrong things that I've done. Soften my heart and give me Your power to "overcome the world" and forgive those who've wronged me with the same openhandedness with which You offer forgiveness to me. Amen.

For Your Journal

_____

_____

_____

_____

_____

_____

_____

_____

_____

From My Journal

Our bags came down the conveyor belt at the Seoul airport with steel cables fastened around them and connected into a small box with a bright flashing light on the side. At our previous stop we'd bought fancy knives to bring home to our boys; but it seems the knives had shown up when they X-rayed our bags as we arrived in Seoul, and the blades were longer than the six-inch maximum one is allowed to bring into South Korea. The flashing light was to tell the customs officers that something was amiss with our bags . . . which was rather disquieting to us!

We had to check the knives into the customs impound office at the airport, then pick them up (after paying a storage fee!) when we returned to the airport to fly home to the US. But on our return, it was quite an ordeal, as a customs officer took the two knives, wrapped in a plastic bag, and walked with us to our departure gate, then carried the knives onto the plane and up to the cockpit to get the airline captain's approval to have them on board . . . then, finally, they were tagged as checked baggage and placed in the luggage hold.

A LOT of effort to get two knives that cost less than twenty dollars home from Asia!

(Author's note: That was the last trip I ever brought home knives for the boys!)

ONE SERMON IN LAOS

But be doers of the word, and not hearers only, deceiving your-selves. For if anyone is a hearer of the word and not a doer, he is like a man who looks intently at his natural face in a mirror. For he looks at himself and goes away and at once forgets what he was like. But the one who looks into the perfect law, the law of liberty, and perseveres, being no hearer who forgets but a doer who acts, he will be blessed in his doing.

JAMES 1:22–25

....

Laos, 2011

We met in a small church building in northern Laos. The church was a simple structure built up over a bare concrete floor. The plastic chairs they used were stacked along one wall, but our hosts pulled four or five of them down into a circle near the front of the church for our conversation. It was hot. The fan blowing in the church moved only the hot air around, doing nothing to make it feel cooler.

We interviewed several Laotian Christians that day, but the one that will always stick out in my mind is "Brother Phan," and the story of the first sermon he ever heard.

Phan was born in a small village in a remote part of northern Laos. After growing up, he wanted to see the world; he wanted more opportunities than a small rural village could offer. And so, as a young man, he traveled to Vientiane, the capital city of Laos.

Coming from a small village, Vientiane seemed huge to Phan. The horn-honking traffic, the thousands of motor scooters, the crowds of people, and the garish lights both intimidated and thrilled him. But the city wasn't as welcoming as maybe he'd hoped, and the economic opportunities he'd heard about weren't quite as obvious as he'd been told. He found himself on the street, wondering when he'd next have something to eat.

Phan had heard that there was a place in cities where a person could get free rice. He didn't know if it was legend or real, but he was hungry enough it was worth finding out. He'd been told, back in his home village, that if you could find a building with a cross on top—and the teller had described what a cross looked like, since Phan hadn't seen one before—inside such buildings they often gave away free rice.

And Phan was very ready for a bowl of rice.

Phan found a church and went inside. As he told me the story, he didn't mention any rice, free or otherwise, at that church. What he did mention is the amazing thing he heard inside that church: the story of a Creator God who sent His own Son to pay the penalty for our sin by dying on a cross because He loves each of us that much.

Phan was mesmerized by the story, and instantly knew He was a sinner and needed someone else to pay the penalty. He spoke with the pastor of that church and prayed a prayer of repentance and committed his life to following Jesus, who had come and died for him.

I don't know whether that pastor bought Phan lunch that day—he didn't mention that in telling the story. What he did mention was his response to the good news he'd just heard.

Phan couldn't bear the thought that no one in his village knew this amazing story, that they had no chance of finding the peace he had experienced, because there wasn't a church in their village. He determined in his own heart to change that.

And so Phan got back on the bus and left Vientiane and whatever economic opportunities it might hold for him. He rode many hours north, back to the small village where he came from. And he gathered the people there, telling them he had learned something in Vientiane they all needed to hear.

Through Phan's early ministry back in his village, sixteen families chose to leave behind Buddhism and ancestor worship and become followers of Christ. Phan brought more than one hundred people to Christ after hearing only one sermon!

Phan continued to grow in his faith, and as he was discipled, he in turn discipled new believers in his village.

But his faith and ministry came with a cost—for him and for other new converts in his village.

Phan was kicked out of the village, along with the other converts who refused to renounce the "foreign religion" of Christianity and return to their former ways. The message was clear: "You can be a Christian, or you can live in our village. But you can't choose both." Phan and the others chose Christ.

Government officials sent policemen and trucks and announced that anyone who was a Christian had to leave the village. Those who followed Jesus grabbed whatever of their belongings they could as they were forced aboard the trucks and driven out of the village. They were told not to come back.

Eventually, Phan and his flock found a new village to live in, but when I met him, he and the other believers were being threatened with expulsion from their new village as well. Phan seemed unfazed by the threats; he'd already seen God provide for their needs after being kicked out of one village. Would God leave them uncared for if it happened again?

By the time I met him, Phan had heard many more sermons, both in person and on the tribal-language radio broadcast that carried the gospel to his people. But I've never forgotten what he did with the very first sermon he heard, how it produced so much fruit in his life and in his village. That one sermon literally changed eternity for more than a hundred people!

I was with my coworker from South Asia several years after meeting Phan and asked about him. My coworker also remembered Phan and his story, but he passed on the news that Phan had died suddenly. Our friend is now reaping the eternal rewards he heard about in that very first sermon—rewards much greater than a free bowl of rice!

FOR REFLECTION

I am the son of a pastor and missionary, and sitting and sweating in that hot Laotian church I found Brother Phan's story instantly convicting. I've heard way more than one sermon. In fact, I've probably heard thousands of them over the past fifty years.

But how often do I walk out the door of my church, college chapel, or camp—or turn off the podcast—wherever I hear the messenger of God, and go on with my life as if nothing has happened? As if I didn't just hear a message of eternal significance for me and for every person I'm going to meet that week? It's way too often.

Brother Phan went out of that church after hearing one sermon, rode a bus for many hours back to his village, and then led sixteen families to salvation. That's making the most of the value of a sermon!

What about you? When's the last time you bolted out the doors of your church seeking someone who needed to hear the message from God you'd just heard? For most of us, that doesn't happen often.

When you walk out of your church this weekend, remember Brother Phan. For your journal, write down a spiritual truth, passage of Scripture, or impactful illustration you recently heard. Now write down the name of one person you'll share it with this week.

PRAYER

Lord, we have so much. We have material blessings and free access to Your Word and messengers of its Truth. Please help us use our freedom well! Help us remember that Your Word is the key to life and willingly, freely, and regularly speak of that life to the people around us.

For Your Journal

From My Journal

Okay, I'm in the exit row, which is the front row of this Bangkok Airways prop jet. The flight attendant just walked me through how to open the [emergency exit] door, and when to open it (when the captain announces, "Evacuate! Evacuate! Evacuate!").

Then she finished the explanation with a smile and said, "But please, do not practice."

PRAYING FOR PERSECUTED CHRISTIANS

The first request we hear from persecuted Christians is, "Pray for us."

Their second request: "Send more Bibles."

Our persecuted brothers and sisters understand clearly the power of God's Word—power to draw others to Jesus Christ, and power to prepare and enable believers to endure persecution victoriously.

PRAY TODAY for Bible distribution around the world, but especially in hostile and restricted nations. Pray every believer in Christ who lives in these nations will have a chance to own their own copy of God's Word.

DAY 37

"WE MISS HIM SO MUCH"

If one member suffers, all suffer together; if one member is honored, all rejoice together. Now you are the body of Christ and individually members of it.

1 CORINTHIANS 12:26–27

....

Southeast Asia, 2019

Her husband had been missing for more than two years, abducted off of the street in Malaysia in 2017 in a choreographed, military-style operation that involved seven vehicles, fifteen men, and took less than forty seconds from start to finish. Pastor Raymond Koh had not been seen since that day, and his car had never been located. Had his family members not gone door-to-door and found security-camera footage of the abduction, it would have been as if Raymond disappeared into thin air.

And now I sat, with my digital-recorder running, holding a microphone in the face of Raymond's crying wife, Susanna.

"We miss him a lot," she said, her tears plain even in the audio recording of our conversation. "The hardest part is not knowing where he is, what happened to him, and how he is doing right now." She went on to explain the heavy price she and their children were paying in the midst of two years of waiting and fighting with their own government for information on her husband's possible whereabouts. Two years of trying to beg, demand, or cajole Malaysian leaders to hold the perpetrators of the "disappearing" to account.

Susanna took a moment to collect her thoughts, to let the tears subside. Her next words were not what I expected: "But we thank God."

She went on to thank God for the love of Christians around the world—expressed in prayers, cards, letters, and emails—that helped encourage her and her children through the long nights and dark days. And it wasn't only the family of God that had stood by her family; it was God himself—"the Father of mercies and God of all comfort" (2 Cor. 1:3).

"God has been very real and personal to us," she said. "I remember the first three weeks, I was very lost, even had panic attacks. But we decided to go for a silent retreat and that really helped me to focus on God, fix my eyes on Jesus.

"One verse that I like is Psalm 46:10: 'Be still, and know that I am God.' I don't need to struggle and strive, but I can just rest in the assurance that He is with me and He will never leave me or forsake me, and that all things work for good to those who love Him and are called according to His purpose.

"Even though the circumstances are difficult, I can see that His grace is sufficient."

Susanna also told me she was convinced God had been preparing Pastor Raymond for the trial he was now going through; she said in the months before he was taken that she had noticed a marked deepening in his spiritual practices. He spent even more time in prayer than usual, and he memorized even more Scripture.

"He was going for prayer walks early in the morning for like three hours," she said, "and, also, he was memorizing chunks of the Bible, passages, and he would tell me; 'Oh, I just finished memorizing 1 Corinthians 15.' I was thinking he is really a great example to follow, and he was very disciplined about that."

She didn't think he necessarily had a premonition that something bad was going to happen. But it was clear to her God was deepening Raymond's faith in the months before he was abducted.

She also thanked God for some of the blessings that uniquely equipped Raymond to live in captivity. She told me that he is a very simple man, perfectly satisfied to have three pairs of pants and three shirts as his complete wardrobe. She also said he's in good health, even playing in a soccer league with teens decades younger than him. She was thankful Raymond doesn't require daily medication that his captors might withhold from him.

Raymond knew he was at risk long before the day he was kidnapped. Several years before his abduction he'd received a small box in the mail. When he opened it up, the box contained two bullets. Susanna had also received unwanted mail: an envelope filled with white powder, which could have been poison. The message was clear: stop your ministry, or else.

Raymond and Susanna didn't stop their ministry. They continued to reach out to the poor and needy, offering help and hope to honor the name of Jesus. They knew the risks, but they carried on.

"Yes, he continued [in ministry] even through some fear and anxiety. But he felt that the Lord called him to fulfill the Great Commission and that means to every tribe, nation, and tongue. [God] does not discriminate, so we just carried on our work with the poor, the needy, and the marginalized, and with God's grace we carried through. It is like almost five to six years we did not have more threats, so we thought everything was okay."

Everything was okay. Until the day her husband didn't come home.

When Susanna went to the police station to file a missing-persons report, instead of asking where Raymond had been that day, or who he was planning to see, or what kind of car he drove, police interrogated Susanna about the ministry work she and her husband were involved in. They showed almost no interest in finding Raymond, but great interest in making sure Muslim Malay people weren't becoming Christians. Susanna finally got up and walked out. It was her family—not the police—that found video footage of the abduction.

I asked Susanna what feelings she had toward the men who had taken Pastor Raymond that day in 2017. Her answer showed an amazing maturity of spirit, but also the battle to earn that maturity.

"From the beginning I have decided to forgive them because they know not what they do, and I follow the example of our Lord Jesus, so there is nothing dark in my heart," she explained, "because I want God to work through me.

"But it wasn't easy. In this two years when I came face-to-face with some of these police who were being questioned at the Human Rights Commission public inquiry, there were times when I feel like strangling them because they were just lying. They were just not cooperating. I remember one time in my car, I was just convicted of my bad attitude towards the police and I had to repent with tears before the Lord that I have to pray for the police. The whole system is riddled with corruptions, scandals, and evil, and I think I need to see the bigger picture. This is a bigger picture that I need to see that God is doing a cleansing in Malaysia and He has to bring up all that is dark and evil so that the light can shine upon it. We Christians, we are the salt and light of the world and we need to pray and need to see God's will be done in Malaysia.

"So, God really had to deal with me first to forgive them and pray for them because they need to know the Lord. If there is going to be transformation in Malaysia, there needs to be transformation in the lives of individuals."

FOR REFLECTION

One thing that has carried Susanna Koh through the years since her husband's abduction is the prayers and love of the body of Christ. For your journal, write about a time when the body of Christ strengthened you in the midst of a trial. Is there a brother or sister in Christ that needs you, right now, to be the body of Christ offering strength and help and hope to them?

PRAYER

Lord, work in my heart in the same way You've worked in Susanna's. Help me forgive. Empower me to love those around me into Your kingdom—even those who've harmed or offended me.

For Your Journal

_____

_____

_____

_____

_____

_____

_____

From My Journal

[Susanna] said they are really trying to keep Raymond's story in the public eye, and also keep up the heat on the government to explain what happened—so the idea of having nine hundred-plus radio stations talking about his case was a big positive in her mind.

Listen

You can hear the interview with Susanna Koh recorded that day at www.VOMRadio.net/Koh.

DAY 38

SLEEPING IN THE CEMETERY

Cast your burden on the LORD, and he will sustain you; he will never permit the righteous to be moved.

PSALM 55:22

·····················

Sulaymaniyah, Iraq, 2008

He laid down, right on the ground. In the middle of the cemetery. Sort of snuggled up to the rocks that marked out the boundaries of one of the graves. "I would lie really close to the rocks," he told us, "to try to have something that blocked the wind. Because, you know, at night it would get really cold."

We had driven to this cemetery specifically so Zarguos could show us how he slept, how he survived, during the six months he was homeless after leaving Islam and following Jesus Christ.

The first time Zarguos saw Jesus was in a dream. He remembers the exact date because it was the night before his mother died. In his dream, Jesus appeared as an incredibly bright light, so bright Zarguos had to close his eyes against the intensity of the brightness. Jesus' message was love: "Don't be afraid. Come to me."

After the dream, Zarguos went first to a traditional church. But he was turned away: "Muslims aren't allowed here," the priest said. He bought a radio and tuned in to Christian programs. The radio station gave an address, and Zarguos sent a letter saying he'd seen Jesus in a dream and wanted to know more about Him and His teachings. He received a reply with the names and phone numbers of Christians nearby; he called and arranged a meeting, and with those other believers he prayed, repented, and committed his life to Christ.

"From the moment I believed, the persecution started," Zarguos told me as we sat in the living room of his rented house. The first person he told was his wife, Chimin. She was the first person to become angry with him. As the daughter of an imam and the sister of another imam, she couldn't imagine her own husband would become an apostate. *What would they tell their families?*

Zarguos's wife's family began with quiet entreaties to return to Islam. But when quiet entreaties didn't work, the situation escalated—first to shouts and threats, then gunfire. Two friends Zarguos had taken with him to help negotiate peace with his in-laws were shot. The three men fled.

Chimin's family refused to allow her and Zarguos's two daughters to leave. It was against Islamic law for her to be married to a Christian, Chimin's father explained, so as long as Zarguos was a Christian, he would not allow his daughter or their daughters to reunite with him.

Zarguos returned home, alone. Two weeks later, as he sat in his living room, someone threw a grenade through the front window. The grenade exploded, but miraculously Zarguos was unharmed. His wife and children had been taken from him, and now his very life was in danger. He fled his own home, and for six months lived in the streets. He would borrow a few *dinar* from a friend to buy enough food to avoid starving, and at night he would retreat to the city cemetery and lie down to sleep.

I asked Zarguos what Scripture verses he had drawn strength from, sleeping in the cemetery, cut off from his wife and daughters. He immediately quoted Psalm 55:22: "Cast your burden on the LORD, and He shall sustain you; He shall never permit the righteous to be moved."

I pushed. C'mon, Zarguos, did you *really* feel like God was taking care of you when you were sleeping on the ground in a cemetery and your family had been taken from you?

"I was feeling that God was with me all the time," he said. "For prayer and for spiritual time, it was a wonderful time for me, best time for me [with] God."

As Zarguos told me this story, Chimin sat on the couch next to her husband. Her family kept her away from him for six months, but after that, she chose the cultural shame of being married to a Christian over the cultural shame of being a divorced woman, and reunited with her husband.

When she returned, she was still very angry with Zarguos. How could he do this? And why? She would live with him, but she wouldn't be happy about it.

But over the course of the next two years, she watched closely as her husband lived out his faith in Jesus, in spite of great sacrifice. He lost his job but kept his faith. He lost relations with his family, but kept his faith. She treated him poorly, pouring out her anger against him. He accepted her anger and returned blessing and love to her. Finally, she couldn't resist any longer.

What changed your mind, I asked Chimin, that Jesus was the truth?

"His [Zarguos's] faith was so strong, and I couldn't control myself, so I decided to follow Him. I thank God for my husband's faith, because his faith was strong, and I couldn't stand strong against his faith, so I decided to be with him."

Chimin knew that if she accepted her husband's faith, her family would completely cut her off. She knew the sacrifice she was making. But what she saw in her husband so impacted her that she would suffer whatever she must in order to have what he had.

I asked the couple what it meant to be together in faith, and now in outreach and ministry. "It is much better," Chimin answered. She said she was still praying for her family to come to faith in Christ, even though in her mind it is impossible. "But," she said, "for God, it is easy."

As we finished our conversation, I asked how people in free nations could pray for them. They asked prayer for a home, because renting was hard for a Christian couple. They asked prayer for a need of one of their children.

"And also we have a message for the church in America," Zarguos said, looking me right in the eye. "Hold fast with the Bible!"

That's a good message for America right now, I said.

"As our experience, the grace of the Bible is why we have this family life together."

It was a two-hour trip back to our hotel, through checkpoints manned by men with guns. And as we drove, I thought of a man who would sleep in a graveyard without his family rather than deny his faith in Christ. And then call it *the best time of his life with God*.

FOR REFLECTION

Seeing her husband live out his faith, even as she was angry and mistreated him, made it so Chimin "couldn't control" herself. She had to have what he had! Have you seen that kind of faith in someone around you? Did it impact you more when that person was in a time of plenty or in a difficult season? Have you told them "thank you" for the example they set?

More importantly, are *you* living your faith in a way others around you are so drawn to Christ that they "can't control themselves"? For your journal, write down what that kind of life and faith would look like.

PRAYER

Lord, thank You that You will "never permit the righteous to be moved." Thank You that You use us—even in our pain and brokenness—to draw others to You. Please help me live the kind of faith that makes people around me desperate to know Jesus—so desperate they can't control themselves!

For Your Journal

_____

_____

_____

_____

_____

_____

_____

From My Journal

We were traveling in a van with some Iraqi Christians who are helping us here. In what seemed like the middle of nowhere, on our way to Kirkuk, we got stopped at a checkpoint. There were two guys in camo with AK-47s, and one of them asked for everyone's ID. When he saw the two US passports, his eyes seemed to light up, and [my coworker] and I were told to get out of the van and follow him.

Having the Americans get separated from the rest of the passengers in the van didn't seem like it was going to end well, and my heart started to beat really fast as the guy with the gun led us over a hill away from the road where we could no longer see the van. I was pretty sure we were about to be kidnapped.

He led us into a tin-roofed little building, where his commander wanted to greet us personally and tell us how much he loves America and how welcome we are in Kurdistan! After I started breathing again, I wanted to tell him how much nicer it would have been if he'd walked out to the van to tell us that! Almost needed to stop and change my pants!

Turned out they were Kurdish Peshmerga troops, and they really do love America!

DAY 39

PRAYING FOR HER TORTURER

Likewise, wives, be subject to your own husbands, so that even if some do not obey the word, they may be won without a word by the conduct of their wives, when they see your respectful and pure conduct.

1 PETER 3:1–2

....

Ethiopia, 2005

"Negasi" was right that his would be a missionary marriage—but he was wrong about which spouse would be the successful missionary!

I met Negasi at a church in southern Ethiopia—an area where a majority of the people are Muslims. The church also had a primary school—up through grade four—and as we interviewed persecuted Christians, we could hear the children and look out the window to see them playing soccer and other games.

Negasi was one of the pastors attending a training seminar at the church—and also there to meet the *"ferengi"* (foreigners) who'd come to visit.

I asked Negasi if he'd been a Muslim once. Yes, he had.

I asked why he decided to leave Islam to follow Jesus.

"It's not me that chose," he answered quickly. "It's Jesus—He chose me!"

Then he told me the story of his missionary marriage.

Negasi had his eye on a young woman, whom we'll call Ife, and one day he was joking with her when she said the words, "In Jesus' name."

Negasi knew that Ife was from a Muslim family, and had assumed she was a Muslim, like him. But he knew what her words meant: this woman was a Christian. Knowing she was a Christian, Negasi said that he took her to his house and forced her to marry him. "By force, he married her," is how my translator explained it. I honestly didn't want to ask too many questions, because it sounded awful. How could a man who would *force* a woman to marry him become a pastor? And what kind of marriage could ever grow out of that kind of beginning? A missionary marriage, as it turned out.

Ife was committed to praying for her husband. No matter what he did, she kept praying for him. Negasi's goal was to re-convert his wife back to Islam. By *any* means necessary.

"I'd been beating her for three years and torturing her for two years, but she was very strong in her faith and never recanted," he said. Even years later, he was in awe of her courage and grace.

Three torturous years into their marriage, Ife's prayers were answered.

One night, Negasi was behind closed doors, reciting the *salat* Islamic prayers. The doors were closed, it was the middle of the night, yet suddenly the room was filled with light, and Isa (Jesus) was there in the room. Negasi said he saw Jesus' wounded hands.

"To whom are you praying?" Jesus asked him, then told Negasi He was far greater than Muhammed, and that He'd known Negasi from his mother's womb. "I'm the One who has been taking care of you until this moment."

When the sun rose, Negasi made his way across the river to a nearby church. It was a Sunday, and church members had gathered for worship. But they weren't happy to see Negasi, whom they knew as a radical Muslim who persecuted Christians—including his own wife.

"What are you doing here?" the church members demanded. "You hate Jesus."

"It is Jesus that brought me here," Negasi responded. An evangelist questioned him further, and was convinced Negasi truly wanted to follow Christ. Before they would pray with him, they explained what it would mean to leave Islam and follow Jesus: persecution. "People will lay their hands on you," they said. "Because you're a Christian, you will be persecuted. They can come to hurt you, and how will you respond?"

Negasi's answer was simple: "Jesus, Who brought me here, will take care of everything. He will not leave me."

On his way home from the church, the time came for his Muslim prayers. Out of habit and training, Negasi knelt down to pray. But instead of the Islamic prayers, he asked Jesus to open his mind, open his mouth, and open his heart to know Him more.

When Negasi told his wife that Jesus had visited him, Ife began to shout "Hallelujah!" so loudly that the neighbors wondered what was going on.

The church members had promised Negasi persecution, and their promise was quickly kept. Within days, a group of local Muslims grabbed Negasi and demanded he recite the Muslim prayer. Because he had studied Arabic, he tried to defend himself from the Quran: "The Quran itself says Jesus is the son of God but Muhammed is just a prophet." The Muslim mob was not convinced. They gave Negasi one week to change his mind and return to Islam. If he didn't, they promised to be back to wage *jihad* against him.

A week later, they were back, and one of the Muslims held a sword over Negasi's neck. The man who had beaten his wife for three years had become a bold evangelist in less than three weeks. "If I die, my son will be a preacher," he told the crowd. "If you scrape my flesh, whoever touches it will become a Christian. And the place where I die, the church will be built." Miraculously, the crowd let him go.

But the threats continued. On another occasion, radical Muslims came to Negasi's house, but he wasn't home. They locked Ife and their son inside the house, then lit it on fire. The woman who had put up with being beaten for three years and prayed her husband into the kingdom of God showed the same faith as her house burned around her. "The God of Shadrach, Meshach, and Abednego is my God!" she shouted as the flames grew. She and her son walked out of the burning building unharmed.

When I met him, Negasi said he and Ife are both evangelists. He reaches out to the men, and she reaches out to the women. They've had to flee their original village, but they continue to share Jesus wherever they go and with whomever they come into contact. Theirs is truly a missionary marriage, though it's certainly not the way Negasi envisioned it would be.

FOR REFLECTION

I would never advise a wife to stay in the abusive situation Ife was in. Yet God used her willingness to return good for evil, and her perseverance in prayer, to change her husband's heart and launch an amazing ministry. Is there an area in your life where you need to show more perseverance in grace and prayer? In your journal or in discussion with a Christian friend, explore an area where you need to persevere even though you feel like quitting or getting out.

PRAYER

Jesus, thank You that even the vilest man is not beyond Your grace. Help me never give up on praying for those You place in my path who don't yet know You—even if they're angry or evil towards me.

For Your Journal

_____

_____

_____

_____

_____

_____

_____

_____

_____

From My Journal

The last guy we talked to [today] was a Muslim who married a Christian girl—by force. For three years, he beat her and tried to get her to become a Muslim— until he had a vision of Jesus saying, "Follow Me." Can you imagine being that wife—enduring years of beatings to win your husband to Christ? Wow! Since he followed Christ, he has been beaten and almost killed—but he is still going about the work.

QUOTE TO CONSIDER

Death is the happiest day of our lives.
We must rejoice in it more than anything,
because it is our arrival in our true homeland.

—Maurice Tornay (1910–1949)[9]

DAY 40

LEAVING
A LEGACY

His master said to him, "Well done, good and faithful servant. . . .
Enter into the joy of your master."

MATTHEW 25:21

. . . .

Halmahera, Indonesia, 2003

For most of my work-related trips over the past twenty-three years,
the best part of the trip is the end. I love coming back home to my
wife and sons! The flights home always seem so long, like they might
never end. Or maybe I'm just impatient to hug my wife, sleep in
my own bed, and unpack both my suitcase and the stories I have
from the journey.

Our forty-day journey together is almost over, as well. I hope
you'll spend some time unpacking the stories we've shared and, more
importantly, the lessons God may be teaching you through the ex-
amples of persecuted believers around the world.

Instead of one last story, I want to leave you with a picture:

Every time I look at this photo, I'm challenged. I took this picture in Indonesia in 2003. This is a grave. But it's an empty grave.

My coworkers and I were on an island called Halmahera way out at the eastern end of Indonesia, in the region called the Moluccas—a region which had seen intense persecution in the years before our visit. The very first people to bring Christianity to the island were a Dutch missionary couple that arrived on Halmahera in the 1860s.

I know almost nothing about this family except that they came to bring the gospel to that island, they died, and were buried on the island, right beside the house they'd built to live in, on a hill overlooking a beautiful freshwater lake. I don't know what denomination they were a part of, how many children they had, or how long they lived there before they passed into eternity. I don't know if they saw islanders come to Christ in droves, if they labored many years only to see one or two Indonesians meet Jesus, or if they never saw a single convert.

I know only that this couple lived and ministered and died on that island. And they were buried in this grave.

It may be tough to tell from this picture (I think you could put a Popsicle stick in the ground on Halmahera, and in six months have a tree!), but their grave is empty now. There are no bones in the grave where that missionary couple was buried.

A couple years before I was there, radical Muslims went on a rampage across Halmahera. Our team saw some of the churches they'd burned. We met Christians they'd attacked and wounded or who'd watched as family members were brutally killed. But the radical Muslims didn't just attack churches, Christian homes, or even living-and-breathing Christians. In the white-hot fire of their hatred and rage, attacking *today's* church wasn't enough.

The rage-filled mob was so incensed by the presence of this grave—more than a hundred years old—that they dug up the bones of this Dutch missionary couple and burned them. They had a bonfire to burn the missionaries' bones and erase from their "Muslim" island the presence of Christianity, even going back to the "source," the first Christian witness that ever existed on the island.

I know almost nothing about this family. But I do know this: that Dutch missionary couple left an amazing spiritual legacy.

The spiritual legacy of that missionary couple was so great that more than a century after they died, the enemy was still mad about the way they lived. He was still mad someone had come and planted the gospel flag on "his" territory. Still mad that he had lost even one inch of ground, even one heart that would now spend eternity in heaven. *How dare they!* More than a hundred years after they died, people pointed to the place where their bones were buried and said, "Those were Christian people."

Dear reader, if Satan is still mad one hundred years after you die about the way *you* lived your life and the witness you were for Christ, that's a mark of high honor, an amazing spiritual legacy! During our journey together these past forty days we've met such people living the kind of lives Satan is going to be mad about for a long time.

Now, day by day and month by month into the future, as long as the Lord allows, we must choose to be such people, to live such lives for Him.

FOR REFLECTION

What do you want your spiritual legacy to be? Do you want it to be one that Satan will still be mad about long after you're dead and gone? For your journal, write about the legacy you want to leave. What will you do *today* to add a brick to the spiritual legacy you intend to build?

PRAYER

Lord Jesus, strengthen and empower me to live for You in such a bold way that it will make a difference for *years* to come and in eternity through the lives of people You touch through me. Help me build my legacy, day by day, action by action and conversation by conversation as I represent You and Your love to all those around me.

For Your Journal

_____

_____

_____

_____

_____

_____

_____

_____

_____

_____

_____

From My Journal

The attackers (Laskar Jihad) came from both the sea and the jungle, so the villagers had no place to run. We probably had twenty people stand together for a picture of those who had an immediate family member die in the attacks. . . .

I'm reading Romans on this trip, and read this today:

"First, I thank my God through Jesus Christ for you all, because your faith is being proclaimed throughout the whole world" (1:8 NASB).

I think that is a good VOM verse—we are proclaiming the faith of persecuted believers throughout the whole world.

ACKNOWLEDGMENTS

The fact you're holding this book in your hand is the fulfillment of a dream I've had for many years. Dreams don't come true without help!

First, I gratefully acknowledge the persecuted Christians I've met and interviewed over the past twenty-three years. Often the things I seek to talk about with them are among the most painful and difficult moments of their lives. Yet they have willingly shared, allowed me to ask questions, and entrusted their precious stories to me. I know such conversations are a sacred honor. Thank you, my brothers and sisters. I hope I've told your stories well.

My wife, Char, has sacrificially sent me out all over the world, and sometimes even gone with me to meet the faith heroes whom VOM serves. She's my partner in life and ministry, and my best friend. There is nobody I'd rather get on an airplane with, or come home to!

Kameron and Kedrick, our sons, have prayed for me, watched out for their mom, and listened to stories I've told after every trip (sometimes willingly!). Now they are men with their own wives, responsibilities, and work. I'm thankful their lives show they love Jesus!

Danielle and Laura both joined our family in recent years, two daughters after so many years of only boys. Our sons chose exceedingly well, and we love both "our" girls!

My parents, Phil and Lucille Nettleton, have modeled a life of service to Christ and His Body. I consider my first step toward working at VOM to be the day in 1982 when our family left the US to serve as missionaries in Papua New Guinea. Since then my parents have served in numerous places and roles, and been on lots of airplanes! Their faithful hearts to serve both God and people continues to be an inspiration.

I wanted to write this book for years, but was never disciplined enough to make steady progress. That changed when I enlisted my friend, former coworker, and fellow Dodgers fan Dr. Sid Webb as my writing accountability partner. He graciously held my feet to the fire; without his help, this book might still be in progress instead of in your hands. Thank you, Dr. Sid!

I am grateful for the love and support of my VOM friends and coworkers:

Cole Richards—my boss, the current VOM president—has been an advocate for this book, for VOM Radio and for me personally. I'm thankful for his leadership.

I am deeply grateful to Jim Dau, VOM's past president, who green-lit the launch of VOM Radio. From the very first episode, Jim believed in the program and supported it (and me)—with words of encouragement and budget dollars. Thank you, Jim.

Chris Robinette helped connect this manuscript with Moody Publishers and worked out all the details on the publishing side so I could focus completely on telling the stories in the best way possible.

Cheryl Odden hired me to work at VOM those many years ago, altering the course of my life by inviting me to join in serving persecuted Christians. She and David Robbins were a great help in strengthening the Scripture, devotional, and application content of this book, and I'm very thankful for their input.

VOM's International Ministry (IM) staff—they wouldn't want me to print their names!—are wonderful partners in ministry and amazing servants of our persecuted family members. On almost every trip you've read about here, IM staff were along as my co-travelers. They worked out details, guided me to the best stories, arranged for translators, provided context, kept me (mostly) out of trouble, and always helped make my job easier. I've loved every chance to travel with and get to know them as coworkers, brothers and sisters, and friends.

Tim, Olive, and Hugh play key roles in the VOM Radio production process. Jeremy Burton has banged the drum for me and for this book. Jon Wilke has served as my publicist, opening doors for me to communicate with tens of thousands of people through various media outlets. Roger Kemp and his team at RK Media (I call them "The VOM Radio West Coast Office") have exponentially grown the reach of VOM Radio and, therefore, the reach of the testimonies of our persecuted family members.

I'm grateful for every member of my VOM family—I wish I could mention each by name. They provide the artwork for each week's radio program, share the stories of persecuted Christians in VOM's monthly magazine through writing, photography, and design, share via social media and at VOM Advance Conferences, pack and send aid all over the world, find plane tickets, process donations, keep our computers running safely, pay the bills, and keep our facility looking wonderful. It's an honor to serve alongside these brothers and sisters who love Jesus and faithfully serve His body.

The team at Moody Publishers has been an amazing blessing to work with. Amy Simpson quickly caught my vision for this book; she's been a champion guiding it from my computer into your hands. Dr. Kevin Emmert edited and sharpened the manuscript, helping each story shine with more brightness and clarity. And Moody's design team created the awesome book cover, which captures the travel motif so beautifully, and the internal pages, which are above and beyond excellent. Thank you to every member of the team at Moody!

Finally, dear reader, thank you! My hope is, after spending forty days meeting our persecuted family members, your faith is different on Day 41. Whatever the cost, whatever sacrifice we may be called to make, Jesus is worthy!

NOTES

1. A. W. Tozer, "Mediocre Christianity," in *Mornings with Tozer: Daily Devotional Readings*, comp. Gerald B. Smith (Chicago: Moody Publishers, 2008), April 15.

2. *The Voice of the Martyrs* magazine, June, 2001.

3. Excerpt(s) from RADICAL: TAKING BACK YOUR FAITH FROM THE AMERICAN DREAM by David Platt, copyright © 2010 by David Platt. Used by permission of WaterBrook Multnomah, an imprint of Random House, a division of Penguin Random House LLC. All rights reserved.

4. Excerpt(s) from THE RAGAMUFFIN GOSPEL: GOOD NEWS FOR THE BEDRAGGLED, BEAT-UP, AND BURNT OUT by Brennan Manning, copyright © 1990, 2000, 2005 by Brennan Manning. Used by permission of WaterBrook Multnomah, an imprint of Random House, a division of Penguin Random House LLC. All rights reserved.

5. Excerpt(s) from THE REASON FOR GOD: BELIEF IN AN AGE OF SKEPTICISM by Timothy Keller, copyright © 2008 by Timothy Keller. Used by permission of Dutton, an imprint of Penguin Publishing Group, a division of Penguin Random House LLC. All rights reserved.

6. Charles H. Spurgeon, "Separating the Precious from the Vile," sermon delivered March 25, 1860, in *The New Park Street Pulpit*, vol. 6 (Grand Rapids, MI: Zondervan, 1964), 154.

7. Taken from *My Utmost for His Highest* by Oswald Chambers, edited by James Reimann, © 1992 by Oswald Chambers Publications Assn., Ltd., and used by permission of Discovery House Publishers, Grand Rapids MI 49501. All rights reserved.

8. A. W. Tozer, "Moral Determination," SermonIndex.net, accessed October 27, 2020, http://www.sermonindex.net/modules/articles/index.php?view=article &aid=4693.

9. John Foxe and The Voice of the Martyrs, *Foxe: Voices of the Martyrs* (Washington, DC: Salem Books, 2019).

Pray

SPECIFICALLY FOR YOUR PERSECUTED CHRISTIAN BROTHERS AND SISTERS

Request your FREE Global Prayer Guide today at **VOM.org/prayer**.